# Curriculum, Instruction and Assessment in Japan

This book provides a comprehensive overview of the history and current status of policy, research and practices of curriculum, classroom instruction and assessment in Japan. It outlines the mechanism of curriculum organisation and the history of the National Courses of Study, and assesses the theories of academic ability model. It also discusses in detail the history of "Lesson Study" – a characteristic method of teacher learning in Japan which creates professional learning communities – and reviews the history of educational assessment in Japan. Case studies on the practice of portfolio assessment in the Period for Integrated Study, as well as the practice of performance tasks in subject-based education, are illustrated to show various examples of teaching practices.

*Curriculum, Instruction and Assessment in Japan* explores:

- Child-centred curriculum and discipline-centred curriculum
- Theories based on models of academic achievement and competency
- Various methods for organizing creative whole-class teaching
- Performance-based assessment in subject teaching and in the period for integrated study

A good guideline for those who would like to use the idea of "Lesson Study" in order to improve their own teaching and management practices and a reference to all working in educational improvement, this book will be of interest to educators and policymakers concerned with curriculum practices or those with an interest in the Japanese education system.

**Koji Tanaka** is Professor at the Graduate School of Education, Faculty of Education, Kyoto University, Japan.

**Kanae Nishioka** is Associate Professor at the Graduate School of Education, Faculty of Education, Kyoto University, Japan.

**Terumasa Ishii** is Associate Professor at the Graduate School of Education, Faculty of Education, Kyoto University, Japan.

# Routledge Series on Schools and Schooling in Asia
Series editor: Kerry J. Kennedy

**Minority Students in East Asia**
Government Policies, School Practices and Teacher Responses
*Edited by JoAnn Phillion, Ming Tak Hue and Yuxiang Wang*

**A Chinese Perspective on Teaching and Learning**
*Edited by Betty C. Eng*

**Language, Culture, and Identity Among Minority Students in China**
The Case of the Hui
*Yuxiang Wang*

**Citizenship Education in China**
Preparing Citizens for the "Chinese Century"
*Edited by Kerry J. Kennedy, Gregory P. Fairbrother, and Zhenzhou Zhao*

**Asia's High Performing Education Systems**
The Case of Hong Kong
*Edited by Colin Marsh and John Chi-Kin Lee*

**Asia Literate Schooling in the Asian Century**
*Edited by Christine Halse*

**Teacher Evaluation Policies and Practices in Japan**
How performativity works in schools
*Masaaki Katsuno*

**Curriculum, Instruction and Assessment in Japan**
Beyond lesson study
*Koji Tanaka, Kanae Nishioka and Terumasa Ishii*

# Curriculum, Instruction and Assessment in Japan

Beyond lesson study

Koji Tanaka, Kanae Nishioka and Terumasa Ishii

Routledge
Taylor & Francis Group

LONDON AND NEW YORK

First published 2017
by Routledge
2 Park Square, Milton Park, Abingdon, Oxon OX14 4RN

and by Routledge
711 Third Avenue, New York, NY 10017

First issued in paperback 2018

*Routledge is an imprint of the Taylor & Francis Group, an informa business*

*British Library Cataloguing in Publication Data*
A catalogue record for this book is available from the British Library

*Library of Congress Cataloging-in-Publication Data*
Names: Tanaka, Koji, 1952– author. | Nishioka, Kanae, author. |
    Ishii, Terumasa, author.
Title: Curriculum, instruction and assessment in Japan : beyond
    lesson study / by Koji Tanaka, Kanae Nishioka and Terumasa Ishii.
Description: New York, NY : Routledge, 2016. | Series: Routledge
    series on schools and schooling in Asia | Includes bibliographical
    references and index.
Identifiers: LCCN 2016014795 | ISBN 9781138892514 (hardback) |
    ISBN 9781315709116 (ebook)
Subjects: LCSH: Education—Curricula—Japan. | Teaching—Japan. |
    Educational evaluation—Japan.
Classification: LCC LB1564.J3 T365 2016 | DDC 375.000952—dc23
LC record available at https://lccn.loc.gov/2016014795

ISBN 13: 978-1-138-60455-1 (pbk)
ISBN 13: 978-1-138-89251-4 (hbk)

Typeset in Galliard
by Apex CoVantage, LLC

# Contents

# Figures and tables

## Figures

## Tables

# Chapter 1

# Introduction

*Koji Tanaka*

## Introduction

The high level of academic abilities in East Asia draws attention from overseas countries. However, to reveal the actual status of the academic ability in a country from various aspects in a multilayered way, it is important to take the approach of the following four perspectives.

## 1 In light of the level of academic ability

Level of academic ability is based on measurable academic ability and calculated by yielding the average of groups in a survey on academic performance. When a decline in academic ability becomes an issue, it mainly means that it is an issue regarding the deterioration of academic standards. Judging on statistical grounds, there is no doubt that the level of academic ability of Japanese children remains in the upper range of groups in the world. However, what we must consider here is that when we focus excessively on the level of academic ability, we overlook other, bigger issues, such as the disparity in academic abilities, the quality and structure of academic ability, and the motivation for learning – issues I would like to discuss in the following sections.

## 2 In light of the disparity in academic abilities

The disparity in academic abilities is, just as the name implies, a viewpoint to see how the academic abilities of children are distributed. Even if the academic standard is high in a country, it doesn't mean that the academic abilities of all children are high. It is more likely that this high level of ability can conceal the presence of the disparities in academic abilities.

This issue regarding disparity was already one of the concerns about academic abilities in the 1970s. The academic achievement of elementary school students in Japanese and mathematics (studied in 1982) provided by the National Institute for Educational Policy Research at that time, which had provided substantial data on this issue, reported as follows (Amano & Kurosu 1992): the disparity between children was more apparent when they entered the fourth grade and when they entered the sixth grade, and the delays in academic performance (those who scored lower than the average score of students in a lower grade) were 24.8% in Japanese and 16.9% in mathematics. Moreover, as the result of the follow-up survey, the delayed status of those children stayed the same without improving even when they became junior high students.

When you look at the results of the latest studies (TIMSS2003 and PISA2003), they have not yet shown bipolarisation of academic performance, which represents a large disparity between academic performances (two-hump camel shaped graph). However, there are still delays in the academic performance in over one-third of children and the disparity stays constant and expands as they advance in their school life. We must be careful not to overlook the issue of academic deterioration resulting from the disparity in students' academic performance by focusing too much on the decline in academic ability based on students' academic standard. And as a current issue related to students' academic performance, it has been pointed out that the disparity in students' academic performance corresponds to the class disparity in Japan.

## 3  In light of the quality and structure of academic ability

The quality and structure of academic ability has been pointed out as an ailing academic ability issue for a long time. It refers to what Takashi Ota pointed out when saying, "The distance between a question and the answer is becoming very close" (Ota 1969), and what we understand as ailing academic ability, which was named by Toshio Nakauchi (Nakauchi 1983). And in this argument, Nakauchi severely criticised the underlying problems and vulnerability of entrance examinations, where students' memory abilities are measured as their academic abilities. In academic achievement tests and assessments, the quality and structure are regarded as the model elements to be assessed to measure students' academic achievements. Therefore, tests and assessment questions are created and analysed based on those elements, which means it is the quality and structure of academic ability that are the essential perspectives to analyse academic achievement tests and assessment.

What are the academic achievement models contained in academic achievement tests and assessments? For example, in PISA2003, to measure students' mathematical literacy, questions are created to see the abilities to set and formalise a subject and solve and understand it in various situations or contexts using mathematics, and academic ability assessments consist of three aspects: content, ability and context. And as one of the aspects to form the academic achievement model, ability is divided into three clusters: the **reproduction cluster** (the ability to reproduce knowledge accumulated through practices), the **relation cluster** (the ability to solve questions in situations closely resembling those in real life) and the **deliberation cluster** (ability to design and implement a strategy to solve question in a situation that is not close to living). These current statuses of the quality and structure of academic ability reveal the problems underlying entrance examinations, which have been pointed out for a long time. And, how to form and assess academic abilities with better quality and depth like the relation cluster and deliberation cluster is strongly recognised as a challenge in educational reform in the world as well as in Japan.

## 4 In light of the motivation for learning

The motivation for learning is a students' attitude to try to learn in a spontaneous and active manner. To stimulate motivation, a good study environment must be developed, and to establish such environment, we must look at not only the classes, which have a direct impact on the motivation for learning, but also other conditions, including home and society, which are related to enthusiasm for living. With the academic ability issues in Japan, it was an IEA study that insisted on the importance and underlying problems of the students' motivation for learning. And unfortunately the latest TIMSS studies also showed the same consistent downward trend in the children's motivation for learning in Japan.

Stimulating their motivation is a challenge in educational relevance, which is led by the questions like "why do we have to study?" or "what do we get by studying such things?" Therefore, without considering this educational relevance and the quality and structure of academic ability, which is closely linked to inevitable issues of educational relevance, one-sidedly emphasizing the competition to gain academic ability can temporarily be effective, but our academic ability issues will not provide a fundamental solution.

Thus, the overview of the current status of students' academic abilities in Japan was provided here in four perspectives: the level of academic ability, the disparity in academic abilities, the quality and structure of academic ability and the motivation for learning. And in terms of the disparity in academic abilities, the quality and structure of academic ability and the motivation for learning, in particular, teachers and researchers in Japan, faced with difficulties, have been looking to solve issues working together in an active manner. Also, *Jugyou Kenkyuu*, which is widely used specifically in Japan as an effective method to improve students' academic abilities, is widely introduced to an overseas audience.

The features of *Jugyou Kenkyuu* (not Lesson Study but *Jugyou Kenkyuu*, the Japanese term written in the alphabet), which draw attention worldwide, are summarised as follows (Stigler and Hiebert, 2002).

(1) Jugyou Kenkyuu is based on a long-term sustainable improvement model.
(2) Jugyou Kenkyuu always focuses on the learning by children and students.
(3) Jugyou Kenkyuu focuses on directly improving teaching methods.
(4) Jugyou Kenkyuu is cooperative engagement.
(5) Teachers participating in Jugyou Kenkyuu consider it as a contribution to not only his/her own professional skills but also the knowledge development of educational guidance.

*Table 1.1* Simple chronology of post-war educational method (Created by Koji Tanaka)

| Educational environments and policies | Year | Educational practices and disputes |
|---|---|---|
| End of WWII | 1945 | |
| The report of the First United States Education Mission to Japan | 1946 | |
| **Official school curriculum guidelines: general edition (draft proposal)**<br>Fundamental Law of Education came into force | 1947 | |
| | 1948 | Core Curriculum Association was formed |
| Criticism of the new education became stronger | 1949 | History Educationalist Conference of Japan <Rekkyokyo> was formed |
| | | **Dispute over Basic academic skills (from the later 1940s to the early 1950s)** |
| | | **Dispute over problem-solving learning (from the later 1940s to the early 1950s)** |
| **Revision of the official school curriculum guidelines: general edition (draft proposal)** | 1951 | The Association of Mathematical Instruction (AMI) was formed |
| | | Edited by Seikyo Muchaku, *Yamabiko Gakko (School echoing the mountains)* |
| | 1955 | Keijiro Konishi *Gakkyu Kakumei (Classroom Revolution)* |
| Sputnik crisis | 1957 | Yoshio Toi *Mura wo Sodateru Gakuryoku (The academic abilities to develop a village)* |
| **Revision of the official school curriculum guidelines for elementary and junior high school education** | 1958 | |
| Economic Council Income Doubling Plan | 1960 | Hiraku Toyama and Ko Ginbayashi *Suidohoshikiniyoru Keisantaikei (Calculation system by the Suidohoshiki method)* |
| | | Kihaku Saito *Jugyou Nyumon (Introduction to Teaching)* |

| Educational environments and policies | Year | Educational practices and disputes |
|---|---|---|
| National Assessment of Academic Ability (Junior high school) | 1961 | |
| | | **Dispute over "Academic achievement model" (the early 1960s)** |
| Economic Council/advocated meritocracy | 1963 | Permanent Committee of the Japanese Society for Life Guidance Studies Gakkyushudandukuri Nyumon (Introduction to create Classroom |
| | | Jerome Seymour Bruner *The Principle of Education* (Original 1960) |
| | | Kiyonobu Itakura, Kazuaki Shoui et al |
| | | *Advocated Kasetsujikken Jugyou Hypothetical Experimental Teaching* |
| | 1967 | Yoshimatsu Shibata et al Gendaino Kyojugaku *(Modern Teaching Methods)* |
| **Revision of the official school curriculum guidelines for elementary and junior high school education** (1969 for junior high school) | 1968 | |
| Issue of Left-behind children came to the surface | 1971 | Toshio Nakauchi *Gakuryokuto Hyoukano Riron (Theory of academic ability and evaluation)* |
| | | **Dispute over Fun Classroom (from the early 1970s to the late 1980s)** |
| | 1974 | Hitoshi Yoshimoto *Kunikuteki Kyoujuno Riron (Theory of discipline driven teaching approach)* |
| | 1975 | Dispute over the academic achievement of Science and Life environmental studies |
| **Revision of the official school curriculum guidelines for elementary and junior high school education** | 1977 | |

(Continued)

*Table 1.1* (Continued)

| Educational environments and policies | Year | Educational practices and disputes |
|---|---|---|
| | 1979 | Masao Nakamoto *Gakuryokueno Chosen (Challenges for academic achievements)* |
| Issue of school violence came to the surface | 1982 | Toshio Yasui *Kodomogaugoku Shakaika (Social studies that move children)* |
| Issue of bullying came to the surface | 1985 | Yoichi Mukoyama *Jugyono udewo Ageru hosoku (Rules to improve your classroom management skills)* |
| | | **Dispute over Education techniques (the late 1980s)** |
| **Revision of the official school curriculum guidelines for elementary, junior high and high school education** | 1989 | Nobukatsu Fujioka *Jugyodukurino Hasso (Mindsents to design classroom)* |
| Dissolving of the Soviet Union and collapse of the Bubble Economy | 1991 | |
| Issue of school non-attendance came to the surface | | |
| | 1995 | Manabu Sato et al *Manabiheno Sasoi (Introduction to learning)* |
| **Revision of the official school curriculum guidelines for elementary and junior high school education** | 1998 | New academic ability philosophy was advocated |
| | 1999 | Edited by Tsuneharu Okabe *Bunsugadekinai Daigakusei (University students who cannot solve fractional questions)* |
| | | Dispute over decline in academic ability broke out |
| Revision of the cumulative guidance report (shifted to the Objective-referenced Assessment) | 2001 | |
| PISA shock (Low level of reading ability) | 2004 | |
| The new Basic Act on Education came into force | 2006 | |
| **Revision of the official school curriculum guidelines for elementary, junior high and high school education** | 2008 | Solid academic ability philosophy was advocated |

These five features are contrasted with problem situations in the United States; it is pointed out that, in the United States, people are more likely to demand immediate outcomes through drastic reform; teachers in the United States are independent and hardly work together; and their approach can neglect children due to their teaching system, where teachers just follow the educational guidance provided and developed by researchers.

In contrast, it is said that in Japan we try to promote educational reform through Jugyou Kenkyuu, unspectacular but long-term sustainable engagement, and teachers in Japan work together and consciously engage in Jugyou Kenkyuu not only as teachers but also as researchers.

The processes of Jugyou Kenkyuu in Japan are introduced as follows. (1) Identify issues, (2) Develop teaching plan, (3) Do a class (pre-Jugyou Kenkyuu), (4) Perform Jugyou Kenkyu and review the effectiveness, (5) Revise the class, (6) Do a class based on the revised teaching plan (Jugyou Kenkyuu within the school), (7) Reassess and review the class, (8) Share the outcomes (reporting and sharing among Kokaiken public workshops).

As described in this book, education in Japan has developed its unique theories not only in the aspect of Jugyou Kenkyuu but also the curriculum as well as assessment viewpoints. This book will be the first book to introduce education and teaching practices in Japan in a systematic way.

## References

Amano, K., and Kurosu, T. (1992). *Elementary students' academic performances in Japanese and mathematics* [Shogakko no kokugo sansu no gakuryoku]. Musashino: Akiyama shoten.

Stigler, J. W. and Hiebert, J, translated by Minato, S. (2002). *Learn from Japanese mathematic education* [Nihon no sansu sugaku kyoiku ni manabe]. Tokyo: Kyoiku Shuppan.

Nakauchi, T. (1983). *What is academic ability?* [Gakuryoku towa nanika]. Tokyo: Iwanami shinsho.

Ota, T. (1969). *What is academic ability?* [Gakuryoku towa nanika]. Tokyo: Kokudo shinsho.

# Part 1

# Curriculum

# Chapter 2

# Historical overview of curriculum organisation

## National control over curriculum vs. school-based curriculum development

*Kanae Nishioka*

## Introduction

In post-World War II Japan, the curriculum basically has been assumed to be something organised by the schools. However, the way and the extent to which the Japanese government regulates the curriculum organisation have been transitioning through several turning points. This chapter will describe the post-war Japanese history of curriculum organisation, focusing on national regulation.

Moreover, the curriculum organisation of schools cannot be established without being supported by teachers' professional development. Therefore, this chapter will also examine how teacher professional development is achieved in Japan.

## 1 Curriculum organisation and the teacher training system

### 1–1 The Japanese school system and the National Courses of Study (NCS)

Before presenting the history of curriculum organisation in post-war Japan, let us describe the basic framework of both the Japanese school system and curriculum organisation.

Japanese schools employ a 6–3–3 system. This means that it comprises six years of elementary school (ages 6 to 12), three years of middle school (ages 12 to 15) and three years of high school (ages 15 to 18). Although elementary and middle school are part of compulsory education, the percentage of students advancing to high school has reached 98%. Secondary schools (a system that combines middle and high school) were founded as a result of the 1998 Enforcement Regulations for the School Education Act, but they remain few in number. According to the School Basic Survey conducted by the Ministry of Education, Culture, Sports, Science and Technology (MEXT) in financial year 2014, there were 20,852 elementary schools, 10,557 middle schools, 4,963 high schools and 51 secondary schools in Japan (MEXT, 2014).

Schools can be divided into state-run, public and private schools. State-run schools are affiliated with national universities. The majority of schools are public schools established by the prefecture or municipality. However, there are quite a number of private schools in urban areas in particular. The middle schools in Japan consist of 73 national schools, 9,707 public schools and 777 private schools (MEXT, 2014).

The curriculum organisation of elementary, middle and high schools in post-war Japan, as a principle, is conducted in accordance with The National Courses of Study (NCS) set forth by the Ministry of Education (MEXT as of 2001). While the first NCS that was developed after the war was treated as a 'draft proposal', the NCS released after the revision of the Enforcement Regulations for the School Education Act in 1958 became 'announced' and had legally binding power. The NCS list objectives and content for each subject along with general rules that constitute the fundamental policies for curriculum organisation. Since Japan employs a government approval system for school textbooks, the NCS serve as a textbook-screening standard.

Moreover, the number of classroom hours for each subject is stipulated by the Enforcement Regulations for the School Education Act. The number of class-room hours for each middle school subject, as stipulated in accordance with the 2008 revised NCS, is shown in Table 2.1. As the table indicates, the current mid-dle school curriculum comprises subjects, moral education, the period for inte-grated study (PFIS) and special activities. For a long time in the post-war period, moral education was not a subject, but a "special subject in moral education" was

*Table 2.1* The number of class hours for each subject in middle school

| Classification | | 1st year | 2nd year | 3rd year |
|---|---|---|---|---|
| **Number of class hours for each subject** | **Japanese** | 140 | 140 | 105 |
| | **Social studies** | 105 | 105 | 140 |
| | **Mathematics** | 140 | 105 | 140 |
| | **Science** | 105 | 140 | 140 |
| | **Music** | 45 | 35 | 35 |
| | **Art** | 45 | 35 | 35 |
| | **Health and physical education** | 105 | 105 | 105 |
| | **Technical arts and home economics** | 70 | 70 | 35 |
| | **Foreign language** | 140 | 140 | 140 |
| **Class hours for moral education** | | 35 | 35 | 35 |
| **Class hours for the period for integrated study** | | 50 | 70 | 70 |
| **Class hours for special activities** | | 35 | 35 | 35 |
| **Total class hours** | | 1015 | 1015 | 1015 |

Source: MEXT, adopted by author

Note: Table 2 for the Enforcement Regulations for the School Education Act (pertains to Article 73).

introduced in the NCS partially revised in March 2015. The PFIS refers to a time in which students themselves set the topic and explore it independently (refer to chapters 3 and 9 for details). 'Special activities', on the other hand, refers to group activities such as class activities, student council activities and school events.

Curriculum development in Japanese schools in actuality is conducted in accordance with the NCS within the framework of the number of class hours indicated within the School Education Act Enforcement Ordinance. Therefore, one can ascertain the trend of curriculum for each period by looking at the transitions of the NCS.

However, how the policies of curriculum organisation proposed in NCS are actualised in a school setting is determined by the selections made by teachers who are responsible for education at school, based on their level of understanding and value judgements. Concerning the NCS, various proposals from a critical standpoint have been made within the Japanese education circle. The reason such proposals are possible pertains to the teacher training system unique to Japan. Section 1–2 will outline this teachers' training system.

## 1–2 Teacher training system

The opportunities for teachers' professional development can be broadly divided into those that are offered in the training process until they obtain their school teacher's licence and those available in the training they go through after becoming teachers. The pre-service training process is carried out mainly by universities that have received course accreditation. On the other hand, in-service teacher training is conducted by various operating agencies. It can be broadly divided into job training that teachers participate in as part of their job and training in which they participate autonomously. Job training can be further divided into administrative training and in-school teacher training (Sato, 2003).

Administrative training is training held by an administrative body, such as a prefectural or municipal educational committee and educational centres. For example, during a revision of the NCS or when a new education policy has been stipulated, training will be held to explain the gist of such new changes. The government shoulders the cost of training, treating teachers' participation as a 'business trip' in which the transportation fee and daily wage issued are drawn from public funds. In regard to statutory training, there is the initial teacher training and training for teachers with 10 years' teaching experience. In addition to these, there are also various types of trainings that are held, including management training targeted toward school principals and vice principals, coordinator training for the head of each instruction department (i.e., the curriculum coordinator) and technical training related to subject teaching and student guidance. In recent years, there have been examples of long-term deployed training where teachers are sent to take a master's course or to a private company for a long period of time. While the Japanese government assists training programmes that prefectural governments hold, the National Centre for Teachers' Development also conducts training for teachers who assume a leadership role and training that deals with the pressing issues related to school education (MEXT, n.d.).

On the other hand, in-school teacher training is a 'practical activity in which all teaching staff members set a common topic as an issue to be resolved in order to realise the educational task as a school that is compatible with their school's educational objectives. The issue is resolved strategically, organisationally, and scientifically by the school as a whole while building upon the coordination between related parties within and outside the school' (Nakadome, 2002). It is said that in-school teacher training in which all teaching staff members participate started in Japan when school-job specifications became systematised in the 1890s and when the class format became established (Nakadome, 1999). As mentioned above, participating in in-school teacher training is part of a teacher's duties.

In-school teacher training is held in various formats, such as a plenary meeting in which all teaching staff members attend, a subject meeting, a grade meeting, and a sectional meeting that is divided according to subjects. The content and method of such meetings can vary as well, including lesson studies, lectures to which an outside specialist is invited and workshops. Lesson studies are widely held in Japanese elementary schools and are starting to spread even amongst middle and high schools. The practice of lesson studies which focus on and aim to directly improve children's learning plays a significant role in the development of new teaching methods and the promotion of shared understanding, in addition to improving each individual teacher's competence. Furthermore, various research results have been borne in relation to the method of running lesson studies, including the classroom record-taking method, analysis of viewpoints and method of improvement (see Chapter 5 for details).

The next subject of discussion is the training in which teachers participate voluntarily. In Japan, it is not rare to see cases where teachers voluntarily participate in training held by private education organisations and universities. In the event that approval from the principal is attained, the teachers will be exempt from their obligation to give undivided attention to their duties and are able participate within their working hours. There are cases when teachers voluntarily participate in training held outside of their working hours (i.e., Saturdays and Sundays). This is referred to as 'voluntary training'. When teachers participate in training voluntarily, they have to bear costs such as participation and transportation fees.

Built upon the teachers' voluntary training, the non-governmental education research movement has been taking place in Japan for a long time. The non-governmental education research movement is a general term given to the study of 'movements that advance democratic, independent, and scientific educational research, held through the cooperation/collaboration between parties related to education (i.e., teachers and parents) and private citizens (i.e., specialist researches from various scientific fields) without receiving any financial support from the government, public organisations, corporations, and labour unions' (Usui, 2002). As it will be discussed in section 2, diverse arrays of non-governmental education research organisations have formed in Japan, engaging in activities such as holding regular study meetings and publishing magazines. The origin of the non-governmental education research movement can also be traced back to the Movement for Civic Rights and Freedom during the Meiji era (1868–1912) and the Free Education Movement during the Taisho era (1912–1926). University researchers, alongside teachers, have participated in the non-governmental education research movement, constructing theories while learning from the practice on school grounds. It is no exaggeration to state that various theories in Japanese pedagogy were generated with the non-governmental education research movement as their foundation. The existence of the non-governmental education research movement, executed as a voluntary/autonomous activity of teachers, is a strength of Japanese education that merits mention.

Therefore, section 2 will outline the history of Japanese curriculum organisation by focusing on the trends of the non-governmental education research movement alongside the revisions made to the NCS.

## 2 The era of the new post-war education

### 2–1 Government policies that propagated the democratisation of education

During World War II, education in Japan was held under the rules of the emperor to promote militarism. Japan was considered to be the country of the emperor, who was considered god, with the Japanese people said to be his children. Education was conducted to spread the philosophy of devoting oneself as a Japanese subject to serving the country, and ultimately fighting and dying for the emperor was the right way of living.

With the defeat in the war in 1945, the Japanese government system shifted to becoming a popular sovereignty, with the Japanese education system changing its projection greatly to aim for democratisation. The General Headquarters Office of the Supreme Commander for the Allied Powers (GHQ) ordered the termination of the subjects of moral training, national history and geography that prominently represented the divinity principle and imperialism. Moral training is a subject that includes moral education, and it was treated as a leading subject during the war. The Constitution of Japan that proposed the renunciation of war and pacifism in 1946 later also proclaimed the Fundamental Law of Education and the School Education Act in 1947.

The NCS was first issued in Japan in 1947. Its general provision was stated as follows: 'Our nation's education is currently moving in a completely different direction from the past. . . . What is believed to be the most important thing is that, despite how in the past there was a uniform leaning to implement the decisions made by those above and adhere to their directions as much as possible, now we come to create various things [in the curriculum] using everyone's efforts, coming instead from those who are below [in the teaching and administrative hierarchy]'. Rooted in the repentance of wartime education, the NCS emphasised the creation and design of the curriculum at the actual place where education was carried out. The 1947 and 1952 editions were each presented as a 'draft proposal'. In other words, they were issued as a reference material (guidance) for school curriculum development and were not a legal mandate.

Another characteristic of the 1947 and 1951 editions of the NCS was the adoption of a standpoint centred on the children. The progressive educational philosophy of John Dewey and others was strongly reflected, due to the influence of the US Education Mission, which implemented educational reform in US-occupied Japan. The curriculum encouraged enriching the life experience of children and fostering citizens who could resolve social issues. Social studies, which was a newly established subject, was stipulated to 'expand and deepen the social experience of youths but centring on the issues of the actual lives of youths, without relying on any of the so-called schools of academia'. However, policies centred on children attracted the criticism that they would lead to a decrease in the academic level.

## 2–2 Autonomous organisation of the curriculum

Under the educational policy that promoted the autonomous organisation of the curriculum across Japan, various attempts at curriculum organisation were actively made by regions, schools and non-governmental education research organisations immediately following the war. Those who took charge of such attempts were those who succeeded the Taisho era's Free Education Movement or the Life Writing Education Movement of the 1920s. The Taisho era's Free Education Movement took place in elementary schools affiliated with a normal school [i.e., a school for training teachers] or private schools in urban areas, after being influenced by the New Education Movement that was vigorous in Europe and the US during the late 19th to early 20th centuries. On the other hand, life writing is an education method that entails having children write prose or poems related to their actual lives and using the subjects of their writing as teaching materials, thereby appealing to how children see, feel and think. It is a method unique to Japan developed by teachers from farming areas within the life writing subject, the only subject that did not have a fixed textbook before the war.

During the early Showa ear (1926–1989), the non-government education research movement was temporarily ceased as oppression by the state increased in association with the implementation of imperialistic education. However, after the war, a variety of study organisations were rebuilt or launched while succeeding the pre-war legacy.[1] In 1946, the year preceding the establishment of the social studies subject, the curriculum development was undertaken all across Japan. The Kawaguchi Plan, which served as a precursor of this curriculum, was a regional education plan that was developed by the city of Kawaguchi-city, Saitama Prefecture, by incorporating the elementary, middle and high schools within the city into the research framework with the support of researchers such as Satoru Umene and Tokiomi Kaigo. Furthermore, the Sakurada Plan proposed in Sakurada Elementary School in Minato ward, Tokyo, emphasised the interests and attention of the children.

The Core Curriculum Association, formed in 1948 (renamed the Japanese Life Education Union in 1953), proposed turning the curriculum into a structure with social studies at the core. It was even referred to as the 'nonofficial Ministry of Education'. In 1950, the Japanese Society of Composition (later renamed the Japanese Society of Writing), pursued a state of education that appeals to the manner in which one perceives, feels and thinks. In 1951, *The Yamabiko Gakko* a collection of essays written by middle school students instructed by Seikyo Muchaku (1951), was published. It received wide attention as an example of practical social studies education rooted in real life, as well as practical life writing education. The practice of life writing had a huge impact on the Educational Science Research National Liaison Council (renamed the Educational Science Research Association in 1962).

Meanwhile, various non-government education research organisations have also been formed from the standpoint of a discipline-centred approach that criticises the child-centric approach. Representative organisations of this approach include the History Educationalist Conference of Japan (formed in 1949), the Association of Mathematical Instruction (formed in 1951) and the Association of Science Education (formed in 1954). These organisations promote the research and development of subject-based education in line with the systematics of academia. It is said that almost all private educational organisations that advance the research of subject content appeared during the 1950s (Otsuki, 1982).

## 3  The era of enforcing the regulations of the curriculum

### 3–1  Educational policies that aim for economic development

The era in which autonomously developed school-based curriculum was encouraged did not last long, due to the reinforcement of the Cold War structure that was triggered by the Korean War. Since the revision in 1958 (revision for social studies took place in 1955), the NCS came to be 'announced' to have legal binding force. Indeed, even in the 1958 revision of the NCS, it was stated that 'each school . . . shall organise an appropriate curriculum'. However, the textbooks that were used in schools were verified by the state, with the request that school education be conducted in line with these textbooks. As a result, opportunities for schools to question the content and arrangement of educational goals or to develop their teaching material without being confined to textbooks died down for a long time, except for a few cases, such as national university-affiliated schools and private schools. Thereafter, the era in which the state stringently regulated the curriculum lasted for a long time.

Another major change to the 1958 revision of the NCS was that a 'period for moral education' that aimed to cultivate patriotism and such was specially installed. Behind this development was the political intention at work to make Japan a fort for anti-communism during the period of developments such as the expansion of the Korean War and the conclusion of the Treaty of Mutual Cooperation and Security between the United States and Japan. Various criticisms were made of the specially installed moral education course, stirring up a debate. These criticisms questioned whether the moral education course might lead to the resurrection of nationalistic education or whether teaching virtues would be an effective form of moral education.

Furthermore, the principle of curriculum organisation shifted to a discipline-centred approach that emphasised the systematic teaching of subjects in order for Japan to become a scientific and technological nation, aiming for the development of academic abilities. The 1958 revision of the NCS proposed a policy aiming to enhance students' basic scholastic ability and emphasise science and technology education. During the 1960s, the income-doubling plan was launched, with an emphasis on developing human abilities even within education policies from the standpoint of stressing rapid economic growth. The National Simultaneous Academic Ability Survey was conducted by the Ministry of Education, and various issues borne out of academic competition became fiercer. The 1968 revision of the NCS had advanced educational content also moving toward lower grades, partially influenced by the modernisation of education that was taking place in the US.

The Japanese economy experienced a period of rapid and dramatic economic growth (1955–1973). The economic growth rate (rate of increase over the previous fiscal year of the real GDP) from fiscal year 1956 to fiscal year 1973 was 9.1% on average.[2] During this time period, the central industry in Japan switched from agriculture to light industry, then to the heavy and chemical industries (cf. Ministry of Health, Labour and Welfare, 2013). As the requirements for being employed at a company after graduating from school spread, the school advancement rate soared rapidly. The advancement rate to high school was 42.5% in 1950 but reached 70.7% by 1965. By 1974, it surpassed 90% (90.8%) (cf. Kimura, 2002).

Combined with the advancement of the education content and the advancement rate, 'children who could not keep up with the classes' (in other words, failing students) became a social issue during the 1970s. As the competition surrounding entrance exams became fierce and issues such as school violence, bullying and refusal to go to school became grave, the harms of the educational style of knowledge cramming were pointed out. In addition, people became aware of the damage of economic growth when the desolation of regional farms advanced and serious pollution problems emerged. The 1973 oil crisis led to the end of the rapid economic development period, and qualitative improvement of education was explored under stable growth afterward (the economic growth rate between fiscal years 1974 and 1990 was 4.2%).

The 1977 revision of the NCS set forth policies that emphasised humanity. Within the backdrop of this development was the impact from discussions at the International Seminar that were held through the cooperation between the Ministry of Education and the OECD Centre for Educational Research and Innovation

(Ministry of Education, 1975), as well as the trends within the US to humanise education. The 1977 revision aimed to make standards flexible by expanding the scope of selected subjects and creating and installing 'relaxed classes', which were left to each school's ingenuity. In reality, the curriculum research on education content did not progress much. Combined with the reduction of classroom hours, the criticism that education content is overly dense lasted until the 1990s.

Additionally, the Ministry of Education appointed schools designated for research and development across the nation in 1976, constructing a system to promote pioneering practical research and development in order to revise the next period's NCS. The achievements of research and development at appointed schools were reflected later in the new establishment of life environmental studies and the installation of the PFIS.

### 3–2 The development of educational method research: Putting the focus on the development of the non-governmental education research movement

Although the autonomous organisation of curriculum had quieted down by the 1960s and 1970s, attempts by teachers acting independently to improve the quality of education continued. When the policy of shifting from a child-centric approach to a discipline-centric approach was indicated in the 1958 revision of the NCS, *Syoshinokai* (the Society for Achieving the Original Spirit of Social Studies) was formed by those who aimed to continue a child-centric approach. On the other hand, from the 1958 revision onward, groups who adhered to the discipline-centric approach criticised the systematics of subjects indicated in the NCS as being unscientific and instead generated research results that advocated their own unique systematics. The '*Suidohoshiki* (way of water course)' by the Association of Mathematical Instruction and the Hypothesis-Verification-Through Experimentation Learning System by the Hypothesis-Verification-Through Experimentation Learning System Research Group are such representative systems. In addition, teachers and researchers who were against the special establishment of a period of moral education formed the Japanese Society of Life Guidance Studies in 1959 that aimed to clarify the correct state for moral education. The Japanese Society of Life Guidance Studies later developed a theory on the creation of class groups that was based on the theory of creating *hans* (small groups), leaders and discussions.

As the state's control on education became strengthened once again during the 1950s, the non-governmental education research movement strengthened its tone of opposing such development. Kihaku Saito advocated developing classes as a role specific to teachers, rather than becoming lost in a political battle. Kihaku Saito, who was the principal at Gunma Prefectural Sabagun Shima Elementary School, devoted himself to the professional development of teachers who worked at the school and theorised the nature of classes and the method to systemise it. The assertion of Saito, who perceived classes to be a reciprocal interaction between teachers, children and the teaching material, has been evaluated as a starting point of the post-war lesson study.

By the 1960s, the non-governmental education research movement's scope was not confined within the framework of subject-based education and had spread to various fields. In conjunction with the rise in the school advancement rate after the rapid economic growth, interest in the method of academic and career counselling in middle schools started to increase. As a result, the National Academic and Career Guidance Research Association was established in 1963. The Japanese Association for the Study on Issues of Persons with Disabilities, formed in 1967, has made contributions such as achieving the 1979 legal mandate to establish schools for children with disabilities.

When the 1970s came and the issue of 'failing students' became a social one, the non-governmental education research movement became revitalised in order to ensure academic achievement. In 1985, the Research Association for the Development of Basic Scholastic Ability and Prevention of Being Left Behind (later renamed the Research Association for Fostering All Children by Developing Basic Scholastic Ability [or Research Association for Developing All Children's Basic Scholastic Ability]) was formed around the ideas of Yuji Kishimoto, who developed the hundred-square calculations. In addition, as theories by Benjamin S. Bloom were introduced (i.e., the taxonomy of educational objectives and mastery learning), the criterion-referenced evaluation movements were borne. The movements aimed at educational improvement by conducting evaluation with the attainment target as the standard (Japanese Association for the Study of the Criterion Referenced Evaluation was launched in 1983).

Even the non-governmental education research organisations that were founded during the early post-war period aimed at creating enjoyable classes from the 1970s onward. Thus, they made modifications to their theories and practice. With these trends in the backdrop, the Section for Developing Classes (which became the Class Development Network in 1996) was born within the Educational Science Research Association in 1986.

By the late 1980s, the trend of perceiving matters through ideologies had weakened for certain, with social movements overall starting to decline. During this period, the Movement for Turning Education Techniques into Rules (Mukoyama, 1985), formed around the ideas of Yoichi Mukoyama, aimed at experimenting and sharing fine education techniques, which attracted many young teachers. However, it drew criticism from those who succeeded the traditional non-governmental education research movement because it did not question the educational value of the educational objectives.

## 4 The era of 'relaxed education'

### 4–1 Educational policies that emphasised individuality and autonomy

As rapid appreciation of the Japanese yen took place, triggered by the Plaza Accord of 1985, the Japanese government expanded the public investment aiming to expand domestic demand in hopes of dispelling international trade friction while promoting Japanese economic growth. Meanwhile, since a policy that lowers interest rates was taken, speculation of stock and land prices intensified. By around 1989, an atmosphere of being carried away by the unprecedented economic boom had spread across Japanese society. However, it later became clear that this was a bubble economy. The central industry shifting from the heavy and chemical industries to the service industries during this period also brought a cultural shift in which value was placed on 'small and light' objects rather than 'large and heavy' objects (Yoshimi, 2008).

During this state, from the late 1980s onward, Japan started to adopt neoliberal educational policies which aimed at developing children's individuality as well as promoting the liberalisation of education. Before this period, the Ministry of Education played a central role in promulgating education policies. However, in 1984, the Provisional Council on Education Reform, which discusses educational issues, was installed in response to the consultation of the prime minister. The four reports by the Provisional Council on Education Reform (1985, 1986, 1987 and 1987) indicated a nationalistic approach that emphasised an awareness of the Japanese people and Japanese traditional culture. Individual-focused education and the implementation of lifelong learning were asserted as globalisation, computerisation and the aging of the population advanced.

Building upon the reports by the Provisional Council on Education Reform, the 1989 revision of the NCS emphasised fostering the desire for voluntary learning and abilities to autonomously handle societal changes. Social studies and science subjects were abolished for first and second grade in elementary school, and life environmental studies was newly installed instead. Life environmental studies are subjects with a strong child-centric tone in the sense that they are focused on making children learn through specific activities and experiences through their lives. Moral education to cultivate patriotism was further emphasised, having reinforced the handling of the Japanese national flag and national anthem ('Kimigayo'). The 1991 revision of the NCS placed 'interest, volition, and attitude' as the primary perspective within its evaluation. It also advocated the perspective of new academic ability that emphasises the fostering of a desire for voluntary learning and abilities to autonomously handle societal changes, rather than the acquisition of knowledge and skills.

In 1991, the bubble economy collapsed, and the Japanese economic growth rate thereafter dropped to 0.9% (between fiscal years 1991 and 2013). The Cold War ending in 1989 and the collapse of the Soviet Union shook the conflict structure between the right and left parties even in Japan.

From the late 1990s onward, the state's control of the curriculum changed greatly. The 1998 revision of the NCS asked for 'creating schools with characteristics', stating that 'each school is to aim at fostering children's zest for living and to conduct distinct educational activities by using ingenuity'. Policies that emphasised schools' ingenuity have been constant since 1998. In 2000, the easing of regulations was propagated, with schools that the Ministry of Education had designated for research and development being solicited by the public and the special-structural reform district being introduced in 2003, led by the Cabinet.

The 1998 revision of the NCS introduced the PFIS, which did not come with a textbook, livening up the opportunity for curriculum development and leading to a great impact on schools. In conjunction with the reduction of classroom hours, subject content was picked carefully, further implementing 'relaxed education', which took place from the 1977 revision onward.

However, in 1999, critics started to argue that relaxed education policies brought about a decline in scholastic abilities. A little while later, the relaxed education policy was forced to make a transition, with partial revisions made to the NCS in 2003 aimed at improving 'solid scholastic ability'. The 2003 NCS presented a policy that stated that NCS indicate the minimum standards and that schools are allowed to teach content above these guidelines. At one point, there was an increase in arguments that called for the return to cramming-style education.

## 4–2 The trend of curriculum research development within school settings

From the 1980s to 1990s, educational issues such as school violence, bullying and refusal to attend schools became serious. Furthermore, there was also an opinion that even if children did not exhibit such problematic behaviour, many children learning at school were essentially 'running away from learning' (Sato, 2000) (in other words, they were not committed to learning). As such development progressed, children's participation in classes came to be discussed vigorously, partially influenced by the Convention on the Rights of the Child adopted by the United Nations General Assembly in 1989 and the legitimate peripheral participation (LPP) proposed by Lave and Wenger (1993). Representative examples of such discussions include the theories of critical thinking learning (Takeuchi, 1994) and learning community (Sato, 1995).

The introduction of the PFIS in the 1998 revision of the NCS revitalised the curriculum reformation across the country. Schools that succeeded the Taisho-era liberal education or post-war new education traditions served as the forerunners of this reformation. Teachers from across Japan gathered for the public research meeting of such traditional schools, sharing the exploratory methods of learning and teaching. The introduction of the PFIS had a major significance in spreading education that encompasses modern issues from various angles, including education on life, career education, human rights education, citizenship education, international understanding education, environment education and disaster prevention education. Furthermore, since it was apparent that evaluating this class with traditional tests would be difficult, it also served as an impetus for the portfolio assessment to receive attention.

Another new development that occurred since the 1990s that merits attention is the trend of education reform led by regional municipalities seen in various areas in Japan. In particular, the initiatives by the Kochi Prefecture that aimed for the improvement of education competence through the cooperation between households, schools and the region and the initiatives by Inuyama-city, Aichi Prefecture, and Shiki-city, Saitama Prefecture, where the education reform was carried out with the mayor and the board of education at the helm, received nationwide attention. It is true that decentralisation reform and regulation easing by the government were behind this development. At the same time, it could also be attributed to the maturity of the citizens in charge of municipalities.

On the other hand, the expansion of economic disparity through the neoliberal economic policies worsened the poverty issue among children. It is worth noting that during this period, practices of volunteers engaging in assisting children's learning spread across Japan.

## 5  The era of globalisation compatibility

### 5–1  Education policy after the PISA shock

PISA 2003, held by the OECD, revealed in December 2004 that Japanese students' reading literacy had declined from the average level of participating countries. This was a huge blow to Japanese people, who have maintained a high level in the international comparative scholastic ability survey. It later came to be referred to as the 'PISA shock'.

From the PISA shock onward, Japanese education policies started to explore a vision of well-balanced scholastic ability while aiming for the improvement of 'solid scholastic ability'. As PISA evaluates the ability to use language, symbols and text interactively, it clearly differs from the perception of academic ability as an ability to memorise or reproduce knowledge and skills. While being influenced by PISA's perception of abilities, the 2008 revision of the NCS perceived academic ability as including the following three factors: (1) the acquisition of fundamental knowledge/skills, (2) the abilities to think, judge and express oneself necessary for resolving issues using one's knowledge/skills and (3) an attitude to engage in learning autonomously.

On the other hand, moral education is moving consistently toward being strengthened. In the 2006 Basic Act on Education reform, nationalistic morality was further reinforced. The 2008 revision of the NCS reinforced the approach of conducting moral education throughout the curriculum.

Moreover, policies that emphasise schools' ingenuity continued to be implemented. In "About the Education Promotion Basic Plan: Toward the Realisation of Education Nation" (2008), a report by the Central Council for Education, various approaches have been declared, including 'The vitalisation of school with the school and the community joining together as one', through the introduction of community schools (School Management Council System) and the school selection system of public schools; and 'assistance toward initiatives through ingenuity from school settings', which promotes making class organisation standards flexible, guidance by learning maturity, installing teachers for teaching a small number of students, and a school selection system in accordance with regional circumstances.

The reform trend of holding the ingenuity of schools and children's individuality and volition in high regard makes one recollect the post-war new education. However, the 2000s reform differs in modality from the post-war new education, since it is advanced under the neoliberal policies that enforce the regulations on the input (targets) and output (results). "Creating a New Era of Compulsory Education" (2005), a report by the Central Council for Education, put forward a 'structural reformation of compulsory education', which aims for the following state: (1) after the target-setting and foundation implementation for realising such targets have been conducted with the state taking responsibility, (2) the decentralisation reform for expanding the authority and responsibility of municipalities and schools will be advanced, along with (3) ensuring the quality of compulsory education by the state taking responsibility for educational outcomes. In response, the nationwide scholastic ability/learning state survey was conducted from 2007 onward. Due to this survey, schools voluntarily made having high grades on the academic survey their goal. As such, there were criticisms that it restricted educational practices.

Currently (July 2016), MEXT is formalising its examination toward the next NCS revision. In October 2014, the Central Council filed for Education a report on making moral education a 'special subject' (Central Council for Education, 2014); and a "special subject in moral education" was introduced in the partial revision of the NCS in March 2015. Furthermore, in On the State of *Standards for Curriculum in Primary/Secondary Education* (inquiry), the following questions have been asked: (1) How do we conceive a curriculum in which education goals and content, learning and teaching methods, and learning evaluation are perceived as one? (2) What kinds of revisions are necessary for subjects and courses, based on qualities and competencies to be fostered? and (3) What is necessary as a measure for improving curriculum management, learning/teaching methods and evaluation methods at each school?

The reason 'qualities and competencies to be fostered' were raised as keywords includes the influence from international debate related to key competency and 21st-century skills. As globalisation and shifts into ICT progress rapidly, the development of human resources and civilians who possess a zest for living in post-modernised society is being investigated.

### 5–2 A new development in curriculum development

From the PISA shock onward, the aim has been the improvement of solid scholastic ability. In the midst of this trend, the focal point of discussion within schools shifted back to enhancing subject-based education. In particular, the proposition of 'schools that teach and make you think' (Ichikawa & Kaburagi, 2007) had a great impact on the 2008 revision of the NCS as something that strikes a balance between learning and exploration. From the perspective of enhancing linguistic activities within classes to improve reading literacy, an increasing number of schools engaged in the practice of community learning (Johnson et al., 1998) and collaborative learning. In addition, the practice example that develops and practices performance evaluation has received attention as something that indicates the future of curriculum development that fosters the abilities to think, judge and express (Matsushita, 2007; Nishioka, 2009; Tanaka, 2011).

Furthermore, a policy to emphasise the development of qualities and competencies was aimed for in the next revision of the NCS. At the same time, there is increasing focus on instruction for improving thinking skills (Kansai University Elementary School, 2012) and active learning (Matsushita & the Center for the Promotion of Excellence in Higher Education, Kyoto University, 2015).

Knowledge for effectively conducting school curriculum management is starting to be accumulated as well. For example, formats have been proposed to analyse the actual state of curriculum management and to consider improvements (Tamura, 2014). Also, teacher training in a format in which teachers can participate more actively (i.e., workshops (Murakawa, 2005) and case methods (Ando, 2009)) are proposed.

## Conclusion

As the above outline indicated, curriculum development in Japan has experienced conflicts between the state and the people at times, while at other times, the two have impacted one another, and the curriculum has developed to this day. The characteristics of the critical examination of national education policies, acceptance of the realities of children at school, learning from academic research results, and the activities of teachers who propose the ideal state of education, including specific practices to achieve such a state, have been continuously updated and are an excellent tradition within Japanese education.

We are currently experiencing major changes of the times, with developments such as globalisation, moves to ICT and global warming occurring. In order to ensure that children have the ability to succeed in the next generation, we need to recognise the ever-increasing significance of learning from practices and theories that Japanese education circles have accumulated.

## Notes

1 The transition of the post-war non-governmental education research movement is described in detail in Ken Otsuki's Post-war non-governmental education research movement history (1982). Furthermore, *The Teachers Who Pioneered the Era: Messages from the Post-War Education Practice*, edited by Koji Tanaka (2005), summarises the characteristics of representative practitioners who led the non-governmental education research movement.

2 Based on the national economic calculation (GDP statistics) by the Cabinet Office.

## References

Ando, T. (Ed). (2009). *Participating/experimenting-type teacher training using the school case method* [Gakko case method de sanka, taiken-gata no kyoin kensyu]. Tokyo: Tosho Bunka.

Central Council for Education [Chuo Kyoiku Shingikai]. (2005, October 26). Creating new era of compulsory education (report) [Atarashii jidai no gimu kyoiku wo souzou suru (Toshin)], Retrieved July 24, 2016, from http://www.mext.go.jp/b_menu/shingi/chukyo/chukyo0/toushin/1212703.htm.

Central Education Council. (2008, April 18). About the education promotion basic plan: toward the realisation of 'education nation' (report) [Kyoiku shinko kihon keikaku ni tsuite: 'kyoiku rikkoku' no jitsugen ni mukete (Toshin)], Retrieved July 24, 2016, from http://www.mext.go.jp/b_menu/shingi/chukyo/chukyo0/toushin/08042205.htm.

Central Education Council. (2014, October 21). "On revisions of the curriculum related to moral education (report) [Dotoku ni kakawaru kyoiku katei no kaizen-to ni tsuite (Toshin)]", Retrieved June 8, 2015, from http://www.mext.go.jp/b_menu/shingi/chukyo/chukyo0/toushin/__icsFiles/afieldfile/2014/10/21/1352890_1.pdf.

Ichikawa, Y., & Kaburagi, K. (2007). *Classrooms that teach and think in elementary schools: A teaching plan that aims for the improvement of academic ability and deepening of understanding* [Oshiete kangaeru jugyo, shogako: Gakuryoku kojo to rikai shinka wo mezasu sido plan]. Tokyo: Tosho Bunka.

Johnson, D. W., Johnson, R.T. & Holubec, E.J. (1998). *Circles of learning: Cooperation in the classroom* [Gakusyu no wa: America no kyodo-gakusyu nyumon] (S. Sugie, K. Ito, H. Ishida, & A. Ito, Trans.). Osaka: Niheisha.

Kansai University Elementary School. (2012). *Kansai University Elementary School thinking development methods* [Kandai shotoubu-shiki sikouryoku ikuseihou]. Tokyo: Sakurasha.

Kimura, H. (2002). The history and prospect of entrance exam reformation: Based on the systemic framework of educational evaluation and the development of the entrance exam system [Nyushi kaikaku no rekishi to tenbou: Kyoiku hyouka no seidoteki wakugumi to nyushi seido no tenkai kara]. In K. Tanaka (Ed.), *New educational assessment theory and method: The challenge to new educational assessment* (vol. I. Theories) [Atarashi kyoiku hyoka no riron to houhou: Atarashi kyoiku hyoka eno tyosen (I riron hen)]. Tokyo: Nipponhyojun. pp. 165–215.

Lave, J., & Wenger, E. (1993). *Learning embedded in situation* (Y. Saeki, Trans.) [Jokyo ni umekomareta gakusyu]. Tokyo: Sangyo Tosho.

Matsushita, K. (2007). *Performance assessment: Evaluation children's thinking and expression* [Parformance hyoka: Kodomo no shiko to hyogen wo hyokasuru]. Tokyo: Nihon Hyojin.

Matsushita, K., & The Center for the Promotion of Excellence in Higher Education, Kyoto University (Eds). (2015). *Deep active learning* [Deep active learning]. Tokyo: Keiso Shobo.

Ministry of Education. (1975). *Issues of curriculum development: Report on the International Seminar on Curriculum Development* [Curriculum kaihatsu no kadai: Curriculum kaihatsu ni kansuru kokusai seminer houkokushu]. Tokyo: National Printing Bureau.

Ministry of Education, Culture, Sports, Science and Technology (MEXT). (2014). School basic survey: The outline of the 2014 results (final value) [Gakko kihon chosa: Heisei 26 nendo (kakuteichi) kekka no gaiyo]. Retrieved January 5, 2015, from http://www.mext.go.jp/b_menu/toukei/chousa01/kihon/kekka/k_detail/1354124.htm

Ministry of Education, Culture, Sports, Science and Technology (MEXT). (n.d.). *Teacher Training* Kyoin Kenshu], Retrieved January 6, 2015, from http://www. mext.go.jp/a_menu/01_h.htm

Ministry of Health, Labour and Welfare. (2013). The 2013 edition, an analysis of labour economy: Employment, human resources, and ways of working during structural change [Heisei 25 nenban rodo-keizai no bunseki: Kouzou henka no nakadeno koyo, jinzai to hataraki-kata]. Retrieved January 9, 2015, from http://www.mhlw.go.jp/wp/hakusyo/roudou/13/13-1.html

Muchaku, S. (1951). *School echoing in the mountains* [Yamabiko gakko]. Tokyo: Seidosha.

Mukoyama, Y. (1985). *Rules for improving classroom skills* [Jugyou no ude wo ageru housoku]. Tokyo: Meiji Tosho.

Murakawa, M. (Ed). (2005). *Recommendation for workshop-type training in which teachers who will utilise it can engage* [Jugyou ni ikasu kyosi ga ikiru workshop-gata kensyu no susume]. Tokyo: Gyosei.

Nakadome, T. (1999). *Revolutionary strategies of school management: Comparative management culture theory between Japan and the US* [Gakko keiei no kaikaku senryaku: nichibei no hikaku keiei bunka ron] pp. 123–124. Tokyo: Tamagawa University Press.

Nakadome, T. (2002). In-school teacher training [Konai kensyu]. In S. Okuda, S. Kono, T. Abiko, I. Arai, K. Iinaga, I. Iguchi, T. Kihara, K. Kojima & H. Horiguchi. (Eds.), *New edition: Contemporary school education encyclopaedia* [Shinban gendai gakko kyoiku daijiten], vol. 3, p. 72. Tokyo: Gyosei.

Nishioka, K. (Ed). (2009). *Ensuring solid academic ability using a 'backward design'* ["Gyakumuki sekkei" de tashikana gakuryoku wo hosyosuru]. Tokyo: Meiji Tosho.

Otsuki, K. (1982). *Post-war non-governmental education research movement history* [Sen-go minkan kyoiku kenkyu undo-si]. Tokyo: Ayumi Shuppan.

Sato, H. (2003). *Outline of the teaching profession: For people aiming to become teachers* (first edited version) [Kyosyoku gairon: Kyosi wo mezasu hito no tameni (dai 1 ji kaiteiban)]. Tokyo: Gakuyo Shobo.

Sato, M. (1995). Toward the interactive practice of learning [Manabi no taiwatekijissen]. In Y. Saeki, H. Fujita & M. Sato. (Eds.), *Invitation to learning* [Manabi eno sasoi]. Tokyo: Tokyo University Press.

Sato, M. (2000). *Children who run away from 'learning'* ["Manabi" kara tososuru kodomo tachi]. Tokyo: Iwanami Shoten.

Takeuchi, T. (1994). *Conditions for school* [Gakko no joken]. Tokyo: Aoki Shoten.

Tamura, T. (2014). *Curriculum management: Action plan to improve academic ability* [Curriculum management: Gakuryoku koujo eno action plan]. Tokyo: Nipponhyojun.

Tanaka, K. (2005). *The teachers who pioneered the era: Messages from the post-war education practice* [Jidai wo hiraita kyosi tachi: Sengo kyoiku jissen karano message]. Tokyo: Nipponhyojun.

Tanaka, K. (Ed). (2011). *Performance assessment: Creating classrooms that develop the abilities to think, judge, and express* [Parformance hyoka: Shikoryoku, handanryoku, hyogenryoku wo hagukumu jugyozukuri]. Tokyo: Gyosei.

Usui, M. (2002). Non-governmental education research movement [Minkan kyoiku kenkyu undo]. In S. Okuda, S. Kono, T. Abiko, I. Arai, K. Iinaga, I. Iguchi, T. Kihara, K. Kojima &H. Horiguchi. (Eds.), *New edition: Contemporary school education encyclopaedia* [Shinban gendai gakko kyoiku daijiten], vol. 6, p. 215. Tokyo: Gyosei.

Yoshimi, S. (2008). *Post-war society* [Post sengo shakai]. Tokyo: Iwanami Shoten.

Chapter 3

# The long debate between child-centred curriculum and discipline-centred curriculum

*Koji Tanaka*

## Introduction

With the defeat in 1945, our education system faced a great change (Tanaka, & Inoguchi, 2008). Reiterating the history of the National Courses of Study as a national curriculum from the present perspective, the curriculum has been organised on an approximately 25-year cycle (around 1950, around 1975, around 2000) in the form of a debate on academic achievement facing competition between child-centred education (focusing on daily life experience) and discipline-centred education (focusing on science and study).

## 1  Debate on academic achievement in early post-war years

In the early post-war years, a series of works rejecting Japan's pre-war militaristic education sparked a reform of the curriculum, which aimed to promote democratic education in Japan. These works included:

- *Four Major Directives on Education* (1945);
- the *Report on the Delegation of American Education* (1946), issued by the General Headquarters of the Allied Forces centred on American occupation of Japan;
- *New Educational Policy* (1946); and
- *National Courses of Study* (1947), prepared by the Ministry of Education, Science, Sports and Culture and based on the abovementioned works.

"General Edition of the National Courses of Study (draft)" prepared for the first time in the post-war era states that "pupils and youngsters must plan a method of achieving his/her goals and "pursue learning by himself/herself through a real experience by reflecting on the result of his/her efforts. Therefore, real knowledge and skills cannot be obtained without activities in which they try to satisfy their needs arising from the goals they set by themselves. To ensure the gist, social studies and independent research were established in the National Courses of Study prepared in 1947.

As everyone knows, this was because the pragmatism (or progressivism) proposed by John Dewey, who positioned the transition from old education to new education as the Copernican Revolution from teacher or textbook-centred to child-centred, had a great impact. According to Dewey, information and knowledge should be distinguished – knowledge comes into existence only when information is subjectified and integrated into children through problem-solving processes. Like this, the curriculum in the post-war period of new education focused on problem-solving learning that developed the independent aspect of academic ability.

However, in a curriculum focusing on problem-solving learning, a strong criticism occurred that it depreciated organisation of the content of education as an objective aspect of academic ability. The debate on problem-solving learning and the debate on basic scholastic ability that started around 1950 are typical debates. From these debates, for example, the core curriculum federation that shouldered new education on a private level started various types of theoretical and practical searching that was interesting from the viewpoint of the present. However, the movement of the age started to transition from problem-solving learning to systematic learning.

## 2 Movement for modernisation in the 1960s

Around 1960, a movement called modernisation became apparent in America, the former Soviet Union and Japan. Its common characteristic was the contention that the content of education should be drastically reorganised to reflect the content and methods of modern disciplines, which should be learned by children. This was premised on the idea that the content of education in schools was outdated compared to modern disciplines that were emerging in the age of the knowledge explosion.

Especially in America and Japan, consciousness of the criticism of progressivism and empiricism and the establishment of an alternative methodology of education were strongly recognised. Reflecting on the movement in the National Courses of Study and denying conventional empirical curriculums, the Ministry of Education, Science, Sports and Culture came up with Systematic Learning (revised in 1958) and Modernisation (revised in 1958).

It is known that Jerome Seymour Bruner had a decisive impact on the movement. In his book *Process of Education*, he focused on structure (for example, "taxis" of biology) as a basic concept of discipline and organised its educational significance as shown below. It has advantages of (1) illuminating the understanding of subjects, (2) enhancing memory, (3) and improving the ability of displacement and (4) filling in the gap between school education and disciplinary knowledge.

Like this, the curriculum in the period of modernisation focused on discipline as an objective aspect of academic ability. As shown in Bruner's hypothesis (that any subject can be taught to any child effectively at any developmental stage while its intellectual characteristic is kept), it was intended to organise a spiral curriculum taking into consideration the developmental stages of children. For example, mathematics and science exemplified this modernisation. In mathematics, new concepts such as sets, functions and probability were introduced, which were taught at early elementary school years.

However, the curriculum of modernisation developed like this produced the result that the rate of choice was extremely low. In Japan, as symbolised by the dropout problem in the 1970s, it was found that many children were failing to keep up with the lessons, demonstrating that the curriculum of modernisation was hardly successful. In 1975, debate on academic ability restarted, focusing on the importance of the subjective aspect of academic ability.

In Japan, another modernisation movement was implemented, which differed from the above-detailed modernisation process developed under the influence of America. It was launched through proposals by private education research bodies that criticised empirical education in the 1950s. One remarkable proposal is *Suidohoshiki* (the way of water course) proposed by the Association of Mathematical Instruction (AMI) (launched in 1951) led by Hiraku Toyama. In 1963, the Hypothesis-Verification-Through Experimentation Learning System was advocated by Kiyonobu Itakura. The results of another modernisation were inherited by the modern age as a comprehensive source that supports a rich educational practice in Japan.

## 3  Shift from relaxed education to comprehensive learning ability

Later, with the National Courses of Study revised in 1977, 1989, 1998 and 2001, the so-called relaxed education policy was developed. One typical case is establishment of the Life Environment Studies and Period for Integrated Study. Among these, the advocacy of a view of new academic ability with an affinity toward a problem-solving curriculum and learning theory was stressed. Incidentally, the description of the National Courses of Study revised in 1989, which vividly shows the view of new academic ability, is cited below. It says that, in future education, it is important to review conventional educational guidance promoted with the emphasis on commonly furnishing children with knowledge and skills and to make the transition to educational guidance in which credentials and abilities with which children can actively find issues, think by themselves and solve the issues by making decisions and expressing opinions independently. That is, the view of a new academic ability advocates a way of thinking that focuses on *interest, willingness and attitude* more than knowledge.

Aside from this, a sensational article, "Extreme Decline in Academic Ability of Students at Todai and Kyodai" was run in the *Weekly Asahi*, published on March 26, 1999. The title, stating that there was an "extreme decline" in the academic abilities of students from Japan's topnotch universities, was shocking. The subsequent publication of "Fraction-Challenged University Students" by economists (Nishimura, 1999) gave the impression that the academic abilities of university students were in peril. It became obvious that the major third wave of the post-World War II academic ability problem concerned university students, with the percentage of young people continuing into junior college or university education at around 50%.

For example, the problem of a decline in the academic ability of university students turned into criticism of the relaxed education policy in the National Courses of Study as its cause. From a sense of crisis, workbook learning was popular (Kageyama, 2002) for improving the basic scholastic ability of reading, writing and arithmetic (3Rs) in the field of education. In response to the criticism of the relaxed education policy, *Encouragement for Learning* (January 2002) was published by Atsuko Toyama, the Minister of Education, Culture, Sports, Science and Technology of the day, with which part of the National Courses of Study was revised in 2003 (guidance formed according to the degree of advancement and constructive learning were stressed), which shaped the administrative process of the curriculum.

A new impact that has not seen before was added to this problem of academic ability (called the debate on a decline in academic ability). This means the concept of literacy, meaning using academic abilities employed by the Programme for International Student Assessment (PISA), an international assessment study of academic ability. Especially in the second PISA (see the figure 3.1 of 2003), Japan had an internationally top grade in the fields of science and mathematics but didn't do very well in reading literacy. Overlapping with the conventional debate on the decline in academic ability, this led to a focus on reading ability in education policy (Tanaka, 2008).

The Ministry of Education, Culture, Sports, Science and Technology announced a programme to improve reading literacy in December of 2005, as the ministry had a sense of crisis about poor PISA-type reading literacy. The ministry describes the characteristics of the reading literacy of the PISA as described below, saying, "It was greatly different from the reading and reading literacy conventionally used in our Japanese education."

(1) Containing not only extraction but also *understanding and evaluation (interpretation and contemplation)*
(2) Containing *use* of textbooks and discussion about the textbooks in addition to just reading of them
(3) Targeting not only contents of the textbooks but also *structures, forms and expressions.*
(4) Containing continuous textbooks, such as literary and explanatory texts, but also *non-continuous texts, such as figures, charts and tables.*

The expression "not only . . . but also" can be thought to describe the conventional characteristic of reading. In addition, this expression does not deny the conventional guidance of reading totally. Furthermore, the Ministry of Education, Culture, Sports, Science and Technology has identified seven concrete directions of improvement in the Guidance Manual on Improvement of Reading Literacy (December 2005) (descriptions in in brackets are summarised by the writer as necessary).

(1) Enhancing the ability to read a textbook wile understanding and evaluating it

   (1-a) Cultivating the ability of understanding and interpretation for any purpose

   (Clarifying for what purpose a textbook should be read and what is aimed at by reading it)

   (1-b) Cultivating the ability of reading while evaluating
   (Critically reading contents and expression of a textbook, rather than accepting it as holy writ – critical reading)

   (1-c) Cultivating the ability of reading while evaluating

(2) Enhancing the ability to write one's thought based on a textbook

   (2-a) Cultivating the ability of one's thought using a textbook
   (2-b) Cultivating the ability of using it in daily and practical language activities

(3) Enhancing opportunities in which one reads various sentences and materials and expresses and writes one's own opinions

   (3-a) Cultivating the ability of reading corresponding to various textbooks
   (Ingenuity, such as reading other works of the same author and reading the same series of books, is required, in addition to familiarizing children with a wide variety of books and not only imaginative literature but also newspaper and science magazines)

   (3-b) Cultivating the ability of expressing one's feelings and thoughts in a concise way
   (In class, opportunities to express oneself not only empirically and mentally but also logically are required)

Then, it is stressed that reading literacy should be built through not only Japanese but also total school educational activities such as each subject and integrated studies.

Hidefumi Arimoto, who was responsible for measures of the Ministry of Education, Culture, Sports, Science and Technology, pointed out that, according to the standards set by PISA, students are required to express their own opinion about what they read, to evaluate and criticise a textbook, to cite what was described in the textbook as the reasons when expressing an opinion and giving a reason not contained in the textbook. He also indicated that it should be shifted (1) from intensively reading textbooks and instructional material from using various written records, (2) from whole class instruction led by a teacher to cooperative learning led by children, (3) from the exchange of questions and answers between a teacher and children to discussions among children, (4) from understanding of feelings and contents by speculation to interpretation of expressive intention by deduction, (5) from non-critical acceptance of instructional materials to evaluation and criticism of instructional material and (6) from expression based on experience and impression to expression based on reading, from which the direction of improvement can be clarified (Arimoto, 2006).

The ability to use knowledge and skills shows developmental aspects of academic ability in response to the influence of the concept of literacy in the PISA, though it started from a point where the basic scholastic ability of the so-called 3Rs declined. The way of thinking stressing the ability to use the academic ability with this basic scholastic ability is typified in that the problem construction of the National Academic Achievement and Learning Status Survey started in April of 2007, sponsored by the Ministry of Education, Culture, Sports, Science and Technology, shifted from Problem A (problem about knowledge; fundamental and basic content) to Problem B (problem about use; problem whose answer is provided using knowledge in a scenario, assuming real life).

The review of the relaxed education policy caused a shift in the view of academic ability from the view of *new academic ability* to that of *comprehensive learning ability*. A report by the Central Council for Education on the National Courses of Study revised in 2008 points out the following five problems about the relaxed education policy in "Concerning Improvements to the Courses of Study for Elementary, Lower Secondary, and Upper Secondary Schools" (January 17, 2008): (1) dichotomy between the relaxed approach and cramming, (2) situation in which teachers hesitated to instruct with too much respect to children's autonomy, (3) insufficient role-playing and cooperation between mastery of fundamental and basic knowledge and skills and integrated study for the course of study and inquiry activities using them, (4) lack of class time for required subjects in present elementary schools and middle schools in order to master fundamental and basic knowledge and skills and to perform learning activities using them such as observation, experiment, writing a report and disserting, (5) insufficient responses to declining educational abilities both domestically and regionally. This means mastering fundamental and basic knowledge and skills and the course of study using them had been depreciated as a result of the relaxed education policy. Instead of the view of new academic ability that had been supporting the relaxed education policy, the view of comprehensive learning ability appeared.

The view of comprehensive learning ability prescribes the basis of the Central Council for Education revised in 2008 and important elements for academic ability as (1) mastery of fundamental and basic knowledge and skills; (2) the abilities to think, judge and express necessary to solve issues using knowledge and skills; and (3) the desire to learn were given as important elements of an academic abilities in the "Summary of the Deliberations in Curriculum" section (September 28, 2007) by the Subdivision on Elementary and Secondary Education, the Educational Programme Section as the original draft of the report by the

Central Council for Education. Furthermore, this is based on Section 2, Article 30 (Goal of education) of the revision of the School Education Act (June 27, 2007). (Special attention shall be paid to making children master fundamental and basic knowledge and skills to lay the basis for lifelong learning and nurturing the abilities to think, judge, express and so on and a voluntary learning approach required to solve issues using the knowledge and skills, which means academic elements were legally prescribed. This shift can be considered to influence the achievement of the reading literacy of PISA (See Figure 3.1).

Problem-solving curriculum and discipline-centred curriculum are summarised, as above. Looking back, mastery type typified by discipline-centred curriculum

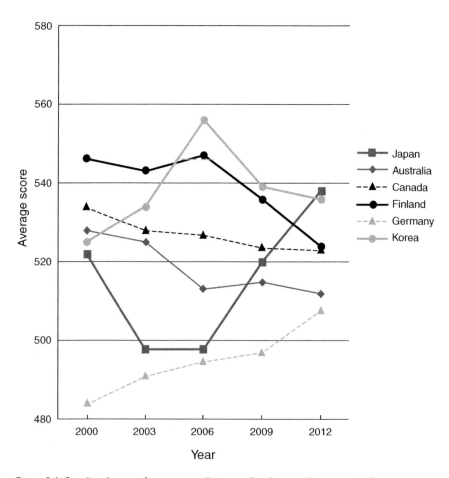

*Figure 3.1* Secular change of average marks in reading literacy (six countries)

Source: The National Institute for Educational Policy Research (2013). *Summary of the Findings of 2012 PISA*, p. 14. (http://www.nier.go.jp/kokusai/pisa/pdf/pisa2012_result_outline.pdf)

and inquiry type typified by problem-solving curriculum can be understand as the objective and subjective aspects of the formation of academic ability, not a form of learning. Of course, compositions of mastery and inquiry differ according to the course of study, depending on its extent of integration, its fundamentality, and its evolvability. However, the history of conflict in the post-war view of academic ability in Japan teaches that it is important for these to interact with each other without separating these and taking a step from the former to the latter.

## References

Arimoto, H. (2006). "PISA-type reading ability leading to zest for living ['Ikiru chikara' ni tsunagaru PISA gata dokkairyoku]". *BERD*, No.6. pp. 4–5.

Kageyana, H. (2002). *Book to gain real academic ability* [Honto no gakuryokuwo tsukeru hon]. Tokyo: Bungei Shunju.

Ministry of Education, Culture, Sports, Science and Technology (MEXT). (2005). *Guidance manual on improvement of reading literacy* [Dokkairyoku koujou ni kansuru sidou siryo]. Tokyo: Ministry of Education, Culture, Sports, Science and Technology.

Nishimura, K. (1999). *Fraction-challenged university students* [Bunsu-no dekinai daigakusei]. Tokyo: Toyo Keizai Shinposha.

Tanaka, K. (2008). *Interpretation of the New Academic Test: Analysis and issues of PISA, TIMSS, and National Academic Achievement and Learning Status Survey and Implementation Status Survey of Curriculum* [Atarashii gakuryoku test wo yomitoku: PISA, TIMSS, Zenkoku gakuryoku gakusyu jokyo chosa no bunseki to sono kadai]. Tokyo: Nipponhyojun.

Tanaka, K., & Inoguchi, J. (2008). *Education to cultivate academic ability* [Gakuryokuwo sodateru kyoikugaku]. Tokyo: Yachiyo Shuppan.

# Chapter 4

# Theories based on models of academic achievement and competency

*Terumasa Ishii*

## Introduction

In post-war Japan, debates about academic achievement have occurred repeatedly during the turning points of the modern era. Koji Tanaka (2008) has categorised the history of post-war debates about academic achievement into five periods: (1) the 'debate about basic scholastic ability' around 1950, (2) the debate about 'measurable scholastic ability' and 'attitude-centred model of ability' in the first half of the 1960s, (3) the debate surrounding 'scholastic ability and personality' in the mid-1970s, (4) the debate surrounding the 'new concept of scholastic ability' in the first half of the 1990s, and (5) the 'debate over the decline in academic performance' in the first half of the 2000s. As shown in the second chapter, it is also possible to categorise these debates more broadly into three phases: the early 1950s, the mid 1970s and the early 2000s. Since the start of the 2010s, the debate on academic achievement has entered a new phase, with keywords being 'qualities and competencies' and 'generic skills'.

In this chapter, I will provide a rough sketch of the issues in the academic achievement debates of each period. Then, I will clarify matters and prospects for academic achievement research in light of the fact that the competency-based curriculum reforms of recent years are making progress.

## I History of the academic achievement debate

### I–I Establishing and developing the question of 'academic achievement'

The theory of academic achievement was born from the counterargument against new post-war education, the context being the circumstances of the post-war era, when it became possible to debate schools' educational content and curricula. In response to critiques that life unit learning had brought about a decline of academic achievement, the educators who advocated for new education argued that, while old definitions of academic achievement such as 'reading, writing and arithmetic' may well have declined, new education was aiming at new academic abilities, such as a 'capacity for understanding life' and a 'life attitude'. From there, it developed into a debate about the relationship between 'basic scholastic ability' (the minimum essentials that should be conveyed to all children) and 'problem-solving academic achievement', which was the aim of new education (the first academic achievement debate).

In the second academic achievement debate, at the start of the 1960s, a debate about conceptual instructions and modelling of academic achievement was launched, the context being the evaluation of instructors' performance, the implementation of nationwide academic achievement tests by the Ministry of Education, and strengthening state control over educational content. The pros and cons of Ryozo Hirooka's academic achievement model became one of the focuses of this debate.

The academic achievement model refers to a desirable state of academic achievement, to be implemented during the teaching process. This is described in daily life as 'understanding the meaning of knowledge', the 'ability to apply knowledge', 'the ability to study and think on one's own'. Whether instructors are aware of it or not, the academic achievement model regulates the quality and orientation of their teaching. In addition, the components and structure of academic achievement model manifests as the behavioural verb of the educational objectives, or as the criteria of the evaluation at the assessment site. For example, the four criteria of guidance records represent one academic achievement model.

While Hirooka (1964) summarised the first academic achievement debate, he described the most desirable state of academic achievement as 'high scientific academic achievement, and living based on developmental academic performance'. In addition, he proposed a model that structured academic achievement in two layers: the 'knowledge layer' and the 'attitude layer'. He described the attitude layer as supporting the knowledge layer (Figure 4.1). However, the Hirooka model was criticised as an attitude-centred model of ability, as indicated below. In his model, the attitude layer lies at the centre of academic achievement; the attitude layer is understood as the tendency of the subject matter to support the knowledge layer and to promote it widely and develop it. Consequently, when a setback occurs in a child's learning, the learner's mindset and motivation is regarded as the problem, without re-examining the problems in the content of school subjects and educational material.

At the same time that Hirooka proposed this academic achievement model, Shuichi Katsuta (1962) suggested a restricted form of teaching academic achievement as 'the ability achieved by studying educational content that is organised such that it can be measured'. Katsuta's idea of teaching academic achievement contained a logic for re-posing the question of what National Courses of Study should be like, by showing conditions that were measureable (the organisation and systemisation of educational content) while responding to the social demands of trying to measure academic achievement. From there, one can grasp the idea that educational objectives and educational assessment are inseparable, and of

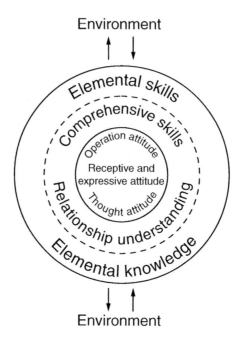

Environment

Environment

*Figure 4.1* Ryozo Hirooka's academic achievement model

Source: Hirooka, 1964, p. 24. Cited by Nishioka, 2009, p. 12

ensuring that assessment continues to happen in order to verify whether educational methods and conditions are appropriate.

Advocates who supported new education tended to discuss general capabilities when it came to the skills to be nurtured at school. In response to this, Katsuta proposed the 'academic achievement' concept, which emphasises 'cognitive capabilities' and underscores the process of transmitting and acquiring cultural heritage from the standpoint of the special skills to be nurtured. However, in Katsuta's argument on academic achievement, there was no thorough discussion about the relationship between the 'knowledge layer' and the 'attitude layer' as proposed by Hirooka, or the relationship between academic achievement and personality.

Various proponents repeatedly had such debates about attitude-centred models of ability. In the 1970s, Tadayoshi Sakamoto and Nobukatsu Fujioka debated the relationship between academic achievement and personality, the focus being on how to interpret Katsuta's definition of academic achievement (the third academic achievement debate) (Sakamoto, 1976). In this discussion, an argument was proposed that positioned personality-related values such as concern, desire and attitude in the academic achievement model, without resorting to an attitude-centred model of ability. For example, Toshio Nakauchi's stage theory (1971) viewed 'attitude' as being cultivated in school education, as the state ('proficiency') in

| Knowledge (cognitive accuracy) | Concepts, images, methods, themes (etc.) |
|---|---|
| Proficiency ||

*Figure 4.2* Stage theory model
Source: Nakauchi, 1976, p. 74

which the student fully internalises educational content and the internalised content comprises part of the student's thought or lifestyle (Figure 4.2). The 'parallel theory' (that was proposed amidst the rollout of the attainment evaluation movement in Kyoto) viewed the relationship between cognition and affect as a parallel relationship. The parallel theory tried to express a state of affairs in which cognition and affect are inseparable and continue to mutually deepen (Inaba, 1984). The stage and parallel theories attempted to discuss the problem of moral education without separating it from intellectual training.

The decline of academic success and low academic performance triggered the debate on post-war academic achievement. The discussion related to measures of achievement such as test results and academic performance. The academic achievement debate developed as a discourse over the most desirable form of intellectual success. The debate contained assertions and values related to academic performance, especially conceptual prescriptions and models of academic ability (Abiko, 1996). The history of the post-war academic achievement debate contains responses to society's demands for results from schools. Pedagogical discussions took place regarding the duties of school education and policies for improving educational practice. The main issues in the academic achievement debates were awareness of the relationship between transmitting and acquiring educational content (the objective aspect) and forming capabilities (the subjective aspect).

In Japan, schools contribute to forming children's personalities. In addition to general educational subjects, morality and special activities are included as part of the official curriculum (special activities are extracurricular ones that nurture children's strength, autonomy and the ability to collaborate with others through group activities such as events, classes and student councils). The twin pillars consist of: (1) Subject instruction that nurtures scientific recognition, mainly through teaching children about cultural heritage; and (2) Life skill training that helps children develop an extroverted personality and to build a sense of democracy, mainly by resolving various problems that occur during individual and culture activities, or in class group activities. The twin pillars have supported general education in Japanese schools. The academic achievement debate clarified the role of subject instruction in teaching children about morality and helping them form their personalities.

### 1-2 Launching the 'learning-centred approach'

In the 1980s, a tendency emerged to reconsider the 'academic achievement debate' in terms of the 'learning-centred approach'. Yutaka Saeki (1982) argued that academic achievement research should be understood as an investigation related to the cognitive process based on the content of school subjects. Such a tendency became stronger, starting with the 'new view of academic achievement' that the Ministry of Education proposed around 1990. In response to the 'new view of academic achievement' and Ei'ichi Kajita's 'iceberg model' (Figure 4.3) (1994) that supported it, several criticisms arose. For example, the new perspective was criticized as being an attitude-centred model of ability that belittled knowledge and saw 'interest, desire and attitude' as measures for grading. Thus, the fourth academic achievement debate was launched (Takeuchi, 1993).

In the 1990s, a tendency to avoid using the term 'academic achievement' became more prominent in pedagogical research and the Educational Science Research Association (1993), which had led the post-war academic achievement debates. Manabu Sato, who had promoted grassroots action research and school reform, played a leading role in this turn of events from a debate on 'academic achievement' to 'learning experience'.

Public trust in the economic value of academic achievement has continued to deteriorate. Sato (1997, 2001) argued that children started to 'flee from learning'. Sato asserted that the value of individual, concrete learning has been denigrated, owing to the fact that the concept of 'academic achievement' has penetrated the practice of teaching. He believes this is a problem. It is not that 'academic achievement' and 'capabilities' really exist, but rather that the 'relationship'

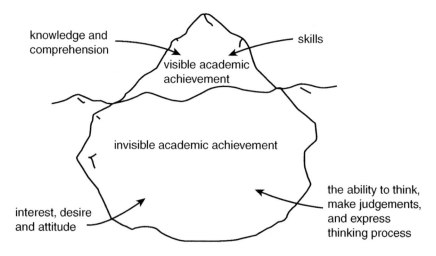

*Figure 4.3* Iceberg model of academic achievement

Source: Kajita, 1994, p. 86

and 'circumstances' of education should be assessed. The concept of 'academic achievement' is used only when rating the 'results of learning'. It is preferable that this concept not be used in the context of daily teaching practice.

In the 1990s, the terms 'learning' or 'learning community' came to be used instead of 'academic achievement' as the key concepts for creating a new paradigm in educational research. Instructors' intentions and technical interventions came to be discussed negatively. Questions related to objectives and assessment were previously included in the term 'academic achievement'. These questions related to the goal of sticking to 'learning', how objectives exist through 'learning' and reconstituting objectives through such inquiries (Tanaka, 2003). These questions ended up being ignored. The intention of continuing to teach common knowledge to all children also ended up being disparaged.

## 1–3 The debate about the decline in academic success and the PISA style of academic achievement

The fifth academic achievement debate evolved from the problem of university students' declining academic success. It developed into a debate about the pros and cons of the Ministry of Education's curriculum policies (such as 'relaxed education') (Nakai & Chuokoron Editorial, 2001). The context involved a sense of unease, and a critique of the National Courses of Study (NCS), which were revised in 1998. The new courses of study aimed to instil in children a 'zest for living' and introduced a 'Period of Integrated Study'. Following the debate on the decline in academic ability, drill studies (such as learning through repetition or guidance according to degrees of mastery) were demonstrated at educational sites. The problem of academic disparities between different social classes and the desire to study became important. Research about creating effective schools that overcome social disparities also made progress (Shimizu, 2009).

In December 2004, the results of the OECD's PISA 2003 were publicly announced. The fact that the ranking of reading literacy fell from 8th place to 14th place caused the 'PISA' shock in educational circles. As a result, the ability to actively consider issues related to one's future and utilise knowledge and skills in the real world (the PISA type of academic achievement) was emphasised, and an approach aimed at nurturing a 'PISA reading literacy' was implemented.

The fifth academic achievement debate questioned the reality of new academic success as it related to a changing society and the methods for nurturing it, while being based on the requirements society placed on schools (in particular, economic circles). The background context was international capability-building competitions. The academic achievement model proposed by the Ministry of Education, Culture, Sports, Science and Technology (MEXT) contained an idea of 'comprehensive learning abilities' whose keywords were 'mastery', 'practical use' and 'inquiry'.

The 'new view of academic achievement' believed that one should not adhere rigidly to common teaching knowledge and skills. In contrast, the idea of 'comprehensive learning abilities' saw the twin pillars as mastering knowledge and skills, and nurturing the ability to think, make judgements and express the thinking process. In terms of these capacities, related keywords were 'practical use'. However, the idea of 'comprehensive learning abilities' received critiques. The abstract '_____ ability' is cited as a decontextualised goal that does not relate to deepening the content of each school subject and formalising the progress of educational practise. The disparity in academic achievement becomes more prominent by focusing on teaching low-performing children the various types of mastery and teaching high-performing children the 'practical use' type (Honda, 2005, Imai, 2008, Koyasu, 2008).

PISA's view of academic achievement sparked theories on capabilities and academic achievement which emphasise the fact that capabilities are embedded in human relationships and learning contexts. The context includes a critical awareness of 'new liberalism' and self-responsibility. For example, Naoki Iwakawa (2005) criticised the fact that 'various kinds of human activities and human richness are being converted into '_____ abilities' in a reductive and skill-oriented way that can be quantitatively assessed' (page 228). Iwakawa proposed that the concept of capabilities centred on contextuality and inclusiveness be re-examined, as well as the responsibility and the potential of responding to others. Yoshiya Tanaka (2005) argued that the proper state of 'strength'-oriented knowledge and academic achievement be re-examined in the context of modern rationalism, while focusing on the quality of 'weakness'.

Hiroshi Sanuki (2009) understands academic achievement as a three-layer structure of 'the layer of basic knowledge', 'the layer of mastery' and 'the layer of expression and creation'. He has demonstrated a way to build academic success that is tied to an enthusiasm for living. This form of academic achievement focuses on obtaining knowledge by tackling pressing life issues for students, rather than taking tests. Tests view competition as the goal and aim to expand the amount of information children remember in 'the layer of basic knowledge'.

The arguments of Iwakawa, Tanaka and Sanuki tend to emphasise the formation of relationships and the desire to learn, rather than cognitive academic achievement. In response to this, Kanae Nishioka (2008), Koji Tanaka (2008) and Terumasa Ishii (2010, 2015) have clarified the model of higher-order academic achievement. They aim to promote living better in modern society, with a focus on intellectual training. They have proposed a form of teaching and methodology to assess it while studying 'authentic assessment' in the United States.

## 2 Competency-based curriculum reform

### 2-1 Issues surrounding academic ability and assessment in post-modern society

In contemporary (post-modern) society, which is considered a global, knowledge-based, or mature society, and in which individualism and mobility are rapidly increasing, individuals are required to have advanced cognitive and social abilities, including the ability for lifelong learning, to respond to problems that are without correct or incorrect answers, while cooperating with others, as residents, workers and citizens. In this context, acquisition of knowledge alone has become insufficient, and society increasingly demands that school education develops abilities for creating and manipulating knowledge.

For example, the OECD's 'key competencies', which are based around reflexivity, are composed of (1) using tools interactively, (2) interacting in socially heterogeneous groups and (3) acting autonomously (Rychen & Salganik, 2003). In addition, in the USA, corporate and education stakeholders defined the '21st century skills' – competencies required to succeed in 21st century life in addition to content knowledge in each academic subject area – as learning and innovation skills (creativity and innovation, critical thinking and problem solving, communication and collaboration); information, media and technology skills; and life and career skills (Trilling & Fadel, 2009). Further, national curriculums and standards in many developed countries are also exhibiting a trend towards clarification of subject-specific and cross-subject qualities and competencies independent of school subject content (Matsuo, 2015). In fact, this trend is visible across primary, secondary, higher and vocational education (Matsushita, 2010).

As discussed above, since the 2000s, Japan has also become conscious of PISA literacy and has begun to value the abilities of thinking, judgement and expression regarding applying knowledge and skills to problem solving. In higher education, the importance of generic skills is emphasised by catch phrases such as 'bachelor's degree ability' and 'basic skills to become a fully-fledged member of society.' For example, the 'basic skills to become a fully-fledged member of society' proposed by the Japan Ministry of Economy, Trade and Industry (2010) are abilities required to actively participate in the workplace and community and are summarised as the ability to make progress (take steps forward and work persistently, even in the event of personal failure), the ability to think critically and thoroughly, and the ability to work as a member of a team (i.e., to cooperate with a range of people for a common goal). In 2015, the NCS tried to clarify not only learning content but also 'qualities and competencies', including general cross-subject skills, and endeavoured to drive a shift towards 'quality and competencies' (competency) based curriculum development and assessment, using systematised instruction and assessment and an entrance exam or higher education linking structure that tests students' ability to continue learning after arrival at university or after exit into work or society (college and career readiness).

In general, 'competency' refers to comprehensive abilities, including social skills, motivation and personal traits, that predict a student's capability in work and success in life. Competency does not quantify 'what you know', but rather 'what you can do' in real problematic situations. To aim for a competency-based curriculum means to re-evaluate the role of schools in relation to the 'capabilities' that society requires and the content of 'academic abilities' that should be developed at school. Within the trend towards intellectualisation and mobilisation of work and social life, the concept of 'competency' tends to be understood in general, cross-subject or-area terms, rather than as occupation-specific. Competency enquires how generic skills should be consciously developed in the lessons of each school subject, or in the education provided by the school as a whole.

The National Institute for Educational Research has proposed a framework for '21st Century Competencies', describing the qualities and competencies to be sought henceforth by school education (see Figure 4.4); '21st Century Competencies' extrapolates the abilities required for cross-subject or-area learning from the qualities and competencies that comprise the knowledge, morals and physical health referred to as 'zest for living'. It is modelled on three layers: focusing on 'thinking competencies' (each individual learning for himself or herself, making judgements, having individual opinions in discussion with others, comparatively investigating and integrating ideas, reaching better solutions and obtaining new knowledge, and then finding the next problem), supported by 'basic skills' (using language, arithmetic and information as tools, and goal-based manipulation of these) and with its use directed by 'practical competencies' (identifying problems in daily life, society and the environment, engaging all one's knowledge and

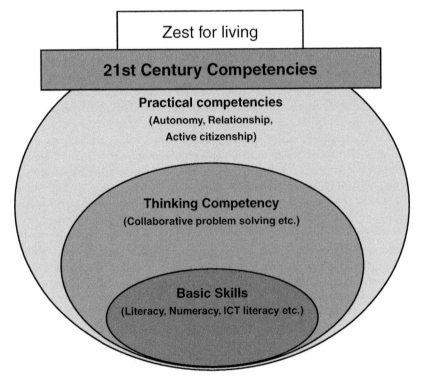

*Figure 4.4* The framework of 21st century competencies

Source: National Institute for Educational Policy Research, 2015.

reaching a solution that holds value for oneself, the community and society, as well as communicating that solution to society and understanding the importance of others and society through collective investigation). Further, the summary of the March 2014 MEXT report of the Committee Regarding Educational Objectives and Content Based on Qualities and Competencies that Should Be Developed proposes re-organising the content of the NCS into the topics shown in Table 4.1.

## 2–2 Dangers of a competency-based curriculum

When faced with the diversification of values and lifestyles, and the increasing mobilisation and uncertainty of society, we begin to want to imagine generic skills that are suited to any kind of society; however, we need to be cautious of a tendency to think that if we can set goals for a given ability (e.g., creative, communicative, or even general human ability), then these abilities may be developed through education. The tendency to attempt to directly teach or train these generic skills and competencies increases the risk of the formalisation and hollowing-out of learning activities and the risk of placing limitless responsibility on school education. Further, if emphasis on qualities and competencies leads to the enforcing of certain individual characteristics or personality traits (e.g., being proactive and extroverted), thus making all daily behaviour the subject of evaluation and assessment, school life may be deprived of freedom and may stifle pupils.

In order to manage these risks while effectively developing the qualities and competencies demanded by contemporary society, we must determine what schools can and should do (i.e., the proper scope of academic ability) and how to manage development of comprehensive qualities and competencies within school curriculums as a whole.

The comprehensive qualities and competencies required by contemporary society cannot be imparted by school, and certainly not by school subject teaching,

*Table 4.1* Objectives and content corresponding to qualities and competencies

---

a) Objectives related to generic cross-subject skills (competencies)

   1 Generic skills, e.g., including problem solving, logical thinking, communication and motivation

   2 Meta-cognition (abilities that enable self-regulation, reflection and critical thinking)

b) Objectives related to the essence of school subjects (e.g., perspectives and ways of thinking unique to school subjects)

   e.g.: Perspectives and ways of thinking on content that answers essential questions of each subject, such as 'What is energy? What is electricity? What properties do these have?' and methods for dealing with and expressing this

c) Objectives related to knowledge and discrete skills unique to school subjects

   e.g.: Knowledge of 'batteries'; how to use a 'galvanometer'

---

Source: MEXT, 2014

alone. For instance, the development of social abilities related to collaboration and autonomy, which are given in the key competencies, has been incorporated into life skill training and extra-curricular activities in Japan. There is a need to reconsider past practices in extra-curricular activities regarding the qualities and competencies required by contemporary society. We must also redesign these activities to complement weak aspects of human development in the out-of-school community (e.g., children's multi-age learning groups) and to nurture life skills required by contemporary society.

So, how should complete school curriculums manage and nurture the qualities and competencies required to live better in contemporary society? Let us consider this by dividing and structuring the qualities and attributes into categories given by various frameworks.

## 3 Frameworks for categorising and structuring qualities and competencies that should be developed at school

### 3–1 Concepts of ability as layered levels and as elements

B.S. Bloom's 'taxonomy of educational objectives' is well known as a pioneering work related to the categorisation of abilities (Ishii, 2011). For example, regarding the objective 'understand Ohm's law', the term 'understand' may be interpreted in various ways, including 'formally remember or memorise' (the remembering level), 'be able to explain interactive relationships between current, pressure, and resistance' (the understanding level), and 'use Ohm's law in daily life' (the application level). Bloom categorised qualitative differences between learning levels regarding specific subject content, conceptualising layered levels of ability. Generally, these educational goals were not fundamentally set as unrelated to subject content. In contrast, frameworks for recently proposed general qualities and competencies, including OECD's Key Competencies, are composed of categories independent of subject content, which conceptualises ability as composed of elements.

When the concept of ability is discussed regarding educational goals, 'ability' refers to either layered levels of ability or ability elements. Figure 4.5 summarises the actual content of qualities and competencies that should be developed by school curriculums as a whole from the perspective of layering; Table 4.2 summarises this with the added axis of ability elements.

### 3–2 Layering of abilities and learning activities

Based on prior research in taxonomy, we may understand approximately three levels of learning depth or quality of academic ability related to a subject's content, as given in the tri-circular model in the 'cognition system' in Figure 4.5. Additionally, methods of assessment and instruction will vary depending on the

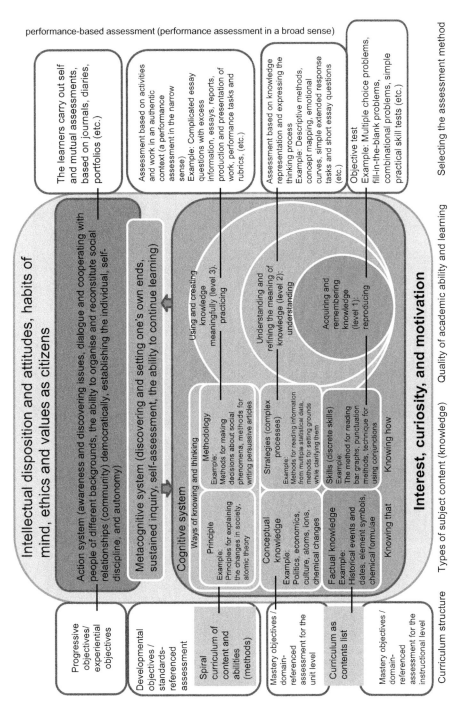

*Figure 4.5* Framework for grasping the hierarchical nature (qualitative level) of capabilities nurtured in schools

Source: Ishii, 2015, p. 22

Table 4.2 Framework for gaining a comprehensive understanding of the elements of innate qualities and competencies that are nurtured at school

| | Hierarchical level of abilities and learning activities (structure of the curriculum) | Elements of qualities and abilities (pillars of objectives) | | | |
|---|---|---|---|---|---|
| | | Knowledge | Skills | | Affective traits (interest, motivation, attitude, personality characteristics) |
| | | | Cognitive skills | Social skills | |
| Subject instruction | Acquiring and remembering knowledge (reproducing) | Factual knowledge, skills (discrete skills) | Memorizing and reproduction, mechanical execution and automation | Learning from each other, constructing knowledge jointly | Feeling a sense of self-efficacy due to achieving one's goals |
| | Understanding and refining the meaning of knowledge (understanding) | Conceptual knowledge, strategies (complex processes) | interpreting, relating, structuring, comparing and classifying, deductive and inductive reasoning, generalising and specifying | | Intrinsic motivation in accordance with the value of the content, concern and desire for the content |
| | Using and creating knowledge meaningfully (practicing) | A complex of domain specific knowledge, with a focus on ways of knowing and thinking (principles and methodology) | Intelligent problem solving, decision making, proving, experimenting and investigating, including abductive inference, discovery and invention of knowledge and objects, aesthetic expression (critical thinking and creative thinking are involved) | Dialogue and communication to conduct projects and working cooperatively | Intrinsic motivation in accordance with the social relevance of activities, belief about subject matter and learning (intellectual disposition and attitudes and habits of mind) |
| Integrated studies | Autonomous sustained inquiry (metacognitive system) | Thoughts and views, world view and self-image | discovering and setting one's own ends, sustained inquiry, information collection and processing, self-assessment | | Intrinsic motivation rooted in one's own thoughts and desires for their better life (keenness), forming one's will power and career awareness. |
| Special activities | Autonomous organising and reconstituting social relationships (action system) | Awareness of relationships between people and the community and culture to which one belongs, methodology related to running the community and maintaining its autonomy | Solving life problems, formulating events and plans, involvement and participation in planning how to resolve social problems | Human relationships and exchanges (teamwork), rules and division of labour, leadership and management, handling of disputes and reaching agreement, independent organising and reconstituting of the sites and community of learning | Social motivation rooted in social responsibility and moral consciousness, establishment of an ethical life philosophy and positionality |

Learning within the contents, tasks, and context given by teachers

students themselves are able to decide and re-structure the learning context and conditions

Source: Ishii, 2015, p. 23

*The classification of the level contains a dotted line in the sections for social skills and affective traits; this indicates that the correspondence relationship for each level is loose, compared to knowledge and cognitive skills.

*The highlighted portions are the elements of the objectives that the curriculum clearly indicates. One should mainly be conscious of these aspects in regards to the respective levels of abilities and learning activities.

*The content of cognitive and social skills should be tailored to each school. The cases indicated in the National Courses of Study should be used as reference materials. In [...] build a formative or curriculum assessment, rather than establish a rating.

intended quality of academic ability or learning. Possessing the ability to solve problems that test the acquisition of discrete knowledge and skills (level 1, e.g., filling in blank spaces with the terms 'population' or 'sample mean') does not entail possessing the ability to solve problems that test understanding of concept meaning (level 2, e.g., the given situation is a survey of 'the quality of sweets produced by a food manufacturer'; the student must determine whether a complete survey or a sample survey is appropriate and state why). Further, possessing the ability to solve problems that test understanding of concepts meaning does not entail possessing the ability to solve tests requiring integrated application of knowledge and skills (level 3, e.g., devising a survey plan for estimating the number of light vehicles in Hiroshima City).

An individual who is skilled at dribbling and shooting drills may not be able to play basketball well. The ability to play basketball well depends on the player's situational judgement within the context of the continually changing match, and this ability is developed by actually playing the game. School education, however, traditionally has students constantly complete drills (knowledge and skill training), meaning that students leave school without having experienced the 'game' (real activities encountered outside school and in their future lives, or activities which imitate the essence of these, i.e., 'authentic learning'). We must pursue rich acquisition of content, concept understanding (level 2) in daily lessons, while consciously securing learning opportunities for integratively using knowledge and skills (level 3) at the end of each unit or at critical points in the term.

In subject learning, where the main object of instruction is 'cognitive systems', teachers generally set a broad framework for content and learning tasks. Because of this, students themselves are not able to autonomously or democratically re-structure the learning context and conditions, and opportunities for truly free and independent learning cannot necessarily be guaranteed in subject learning singly. Regarding the school curriculum as a whole, however, we may find such learning opportunities. In integrated study, students are sometimes asked to set their own tasks (i.e., using meta-cognitive systems). Further, in extra-curricular activities such as 'special activities', students collaboratively construct and reconstruct the context of relationships and rules in their learning community (i.e., using action systems). Action systems set the stage for, and the direction of, cognitive system learning, and conversely, cognitive systems give clear direction and depth of thought to action system learning, through development of recognition and intelligence.

By positioning affective elements behind these 'cognitive systems', 'meta-cognitive systems' and 'action systems', Figure 4.3 shows that cognitive learning, autonomous inquiry and democratic and collaborative activities are supported by interest and curiosity in, and motivation for, content and activities, while they are directed by intellectual attitude, habits of mind and ethics and values as citizens. Simultaneously, cognitive, meta-cognitive and action systems learning also have affective impact through mutual interaction.

### 3–3 Overview of the qualities and competencies that should be developed at school

Regardless of differences in qualitative level of ability, learning includes some form of dialogue between three axes: the objective world, others and oneself. As a result of this ongoing dialogue, the individual develops and acquires some recognised content and methods or skills. Skills may be structured based on the three axes of this dialogue (cognitive dialogue with the objective world, social dialogue with oneself and social dialogue with others). Further, some affective change due to learning occurs through effects of one's community's norms and culture, regardless of learning type. Table 4.2 gives an example of the central relevant knowledge, skills and affective traits – that is, elements of qualities and competencies – for each layer of ability and learning.

Even acquisition of knowledge and skills (level 1) causes the formation of some skill and the experience of some emotion; learning which makes integrative use of knowledge and skills (level 3) is intimately related to the deepening of content learning. The type of knowledge and skills primarily required varies depending on the level of learning, however. The tri-circular model in Figure 4.5 shows the correlation between quality of academic ability or learning and subject content type. It shows that content may be arranged into two types – 'knowing that' and 'knowing how' – and that each type corresponds to one of the three levels of academic ability or learning, from fragmented specific knowledge to general knowledge. In order for activities and discussions conducted with the aim of understanding and applying knowledge to become activities of truly deep thinking without falling into the trap of activism, subject content must have a clear focus on the general concepts and principles that encompass and structure this knowledge as elements, rather than fragmented knowledge, such as factual knowledge or discrete skills.

Additionally, regarding the qualitative level of academic ability or learning, the question is not whether to develop thinking ability, but rather what level of thinking ability to develop. The development of thinking ability in traditional Japanese subject instruction involved rich discovery learning of fundamental concepts and developing level 2 thinking that promoted the structuring of knowledge (understanding-oriented learning, i.e., interpreting, relating, structuring, comparing and classifying, deductive and inductive reasoning, generalising and specifying) within this process.

However, if discrete content such as 'line graphs' and 'column graphs' is acquired accumulatively, students will lack experience selecting which graph to use for a given purpose or situation, regardless of how richly students learn each of these. We must therefore secure independent opportunities for students to use level 3 thinking (application-oriented thinking, e.g., problem solving, decision making, proving, experimenting and investigating, including abductive inference and discovery and invention of knowledge and objects) to integrate discrete knowledge and skills in response to real world contexts.

Regarding this difference between levels of thinking, Bloom's division of problem-solving thinking into two levels – 'application' (problems that may be solved through application of a specific solution method) and 'synthesis' (problems where there is no single clear and straightforward solution method, and which may require writing essays, devising plans, or collectively engaging one's known knowledge and skills) – is suggestive. In Japan, where it has traditionally been important for lessons to focus on students' 'knowing and understanding' existing content, the majority of practical tasks have been 'application' tasks. However, developing the ability to create one's own solutions requires occasionally working on 'synthesis' tasks.

Where the acquisition and understanding of knowledge and skills (levels 1 and 2) is the main aim, there are few problems with a content (facts, skills and concepts) based curriculum. By contrast, more goal-conscious and compound level 3 learning involves longer task investigation times and a longer interval between the question and answer. This then requires conscious instruction of thinking processes themselves. Hence, precisely because level 3 academic ability and learning are pursued, not only content but also cognitive and social skills need to be clarified in the curriculum.

Further, experience gained through daily school life and affairs is more effective regarding students gradually noticing their own way of living by themselves – not through planned instruction of knowledge and skills by teachers, but rather through whole-character building experiences that cannot be programmed into a curriculum. In this way, increasingly integrated levels of layered ability shift the curriculum from a basis in content to one in ability, and then in personality traits, and increase the generativity of objectives and assessment.

In this way, areas of a curriculum may be constructed with a view to ability layering, and methods of instruction and assessment and a format of curriculum structuring may be adopted that are tailored to each layered level. Further, for layered levels above level 3, the content of qualities and competencies are specified separately to subject content in the curriculum. However, simply separating content from qualities and competencies in the curriculum in this way means we must beware of causing the learning process to formulaically drill discrete cognitive and social skills. It is important to organise goal-conscious holistic activities (authentic learning) that automatically encourage integrated development of knowledge, skills and attitudes within contexts that necessitate thinking and acting.

## Conclusion

I would like to reiterate the point that if we are to ensure the rich learning and effective upbringing of children, the 'competency' requirements of adult society cannot be transposed unchanged into 'academic abilities' to be developed in school education. That adult society requires creativity through the use of ICT, or dialogue with a variety of others, does not entail that we should engage in the simplistic thinking that all aspects of school education at all stages of development should emphasise such forms of activity and communication. Children gradually build their frameworks of recognition and basic thinking identity by deepening their constant inner dialogue with culture, within stable relationships. We need to be aware of the significance of this silent learning, and of the silences and intervals created by deep thinking.

Of course, at the secondary and higher education stages, there is potential for making school learning something richer, where students are able to experience the meaning of learning, through rethinking how learning at school should be, based on an awareness of the learning demanded by society. Nonetheless, fundamental physical and mental functions are formed in primary education. We must not ignore this developmental stage and bring adult society into school for the sake of borderless thinking and a fluid relationship with that society, as this may impede concept formation and identity development.

Rather than focusing on the needs of the economic world and civil society, and therefore rushing to socialise or train children into these lifestyles, we should develop the human cores children need to avoid being swept away by society in the future – the means by which they may protect their humanity. In this way, through ensuring that learning both links to social participation and raises acculturated human beings, we may develop children's abilities to not only adapt to and survive in society, but also protect their identity and well-being within that society.

## References

Abiko, T. (1996). *New perspectives on academic ability and basic scholastic ability* [Shingakuryokukan to kisogakuryoku]. Tokyo: Meiji Tosho.

Educational Science Research Association. (1993). *Contemporary society and education 4: Knowledge and learning* [Gendai shakai to kyouiku 4 chi to manabi]. Tokyo: Otsuki Shoten.

Hirooka, R. (1964). What are academic ability and basic scholastic ability? High academic ability, live academic ability [Gakuryoku, kisogakuryoku to ha nanika – takai gakuryoku, ikita gakryoku]. *Contemporary education studies* [Gendai kyouikugaku]. Feb. 1964 extra edition, pp. 5–32.

Honda, Y. (2005). *Pluralising 'ability' and Japanese society: Within hyper-meritocratisation* [Tagenka suru nouryoku to nihon shakai – haipaa meritokurashiika no naka de]. Tokyo: NTT Publishing.

Imai, Y. (2008). How should we define 'academic ability' in a globalized world of hidden realities? [Gakuryoku wo dou toraeru ka – genjitsu ga mienai guroobaruka no naka de]. In S. Tanaka (Ed). *Towards global learning* [Guroobaru na manabi he]. Tokyo: Toshindo, pp. 105–37.

Inaba, H. (1984). *Academic ability issues and achievement evaluation* [Gakuryoku mondai to toutatsudo hyouka]. Vol. 2, Tokyo: Ayumi Shuppan.

Ishii, T. (2010). Current discussions of academic ability: Debating academic ability in post-modern society [Gakuryoku rongi no genzai: posuto kindai shakai ni okeru gakuryoku no ronjikata]. In K. Matsushita (Ed). *Will 'new abilities' change education?* [Atarashii nouryoku ha kyouiku wo kaeru ka]. Kyoto: Minerva Shobo, pp. 141–78.

Ishii, T. (2011). *Development of theories on educational objectives and assessment in the United States of America* [Gendai Amerika ni okeru gakuryoku keisei ron no tenkai]. Tokyo: Toshindo.

Ishii, T. (2015). *What academic abilities and learning are needed today? The light and shadow of competency-based curricula* [Ima motomerareru gakuryoku to manabi to ha – conpetenshii beesu no karikyuramu no hikari to kage]. Tokyo: Nippon Hyojun.

Iwakawa, N. (2005). Deconstructing 'ability' in education: From 'self-actualization' to 'response-ability' [Kyouiku ni okeru chikara no datsukouchiku – jikojitsugen kara outoukanousei he]. In Y. Kudomi and T. Tanaka (Eds). *Academic ability creating hope* [Kibou wo tumugu gakuryoku]. Tokyo: Akashi Shoten, pp. 220–47.

Japan Ministry of Economy, Trade and Industry. (Eds). (2010). *A guide to developing basic skills to become a fully-fledged member of society* [Shakaijin kisoryoku ikusei no tebiki]. Tokyo: Kawai-juku.

Kajita, E. (1994). *Theories of evaluation in education: Changes in academic ability and evaluation perspectives* [Kyouiku ni okeru hyouka no riron: Gakuryokukan/ hyoukakan no tenkan]. Tokyo: Kaneko Shobo.

Katsuta, S. (1962). What is academic ability? [Gakuryoku to ha nanika]. *Education* [Kyouiku], Vol. 12, No. 7, pp. 10–15.

Koyasu, J. (2008). What are 'car wheels'? Issues in reliable acquisition and application [Kuruma no ryourin to ha nanika – kakujitsu na shuutoku to katsuyou no mondaiten]. In T. Takeuchi (Ed). *Perspectives for reading the national courses of study 2008* [2008-nen-ban gakushuu shidouyouryou wo yomu shiten]. Tokyo: Hakutakusha, pp. 27–38.

Matsuo, T. (2015). *What are 21st century skills? International comparison of competency-based educational reform* [21-seiki-gata sukiru to ha nanika – conpetenshii ni moto-zuku kyouiku kaikaku no kokusai hikaku]. Tokyo: Akashi Shoten.

Matsushita, K. (2010). *Will 'new abilities' change education? Academic ability, literacy, and competency* [Atarashii nouryoku ha kyouiku wo kaeru ka – Gakuryou, riterashii, conpetenshii]. Kkyoto: Minerva Shobo.

MEXT. (2014). *MEXT report of the committee regarding educational objectives and content based on qualities and competencies that should be developed* [Ikusei subeki shishitsu nouryoku wo humaeta mokuhyo naiyo to hyoka no arikata ni kansuru kentoukai ronten seiri], (http://www.mext.go.jp/component/b_menu/shingi/toushin/__icsFiles/afieldfile/2014/06/03/1346335_01_1.pdf).

Nakai, K., & Chuokoron Editorial. (Eds). (2001). *Debates and the collapse of academic ability* [Ronsou/gakuryoku houkai]. Tokyo: Chuokoron.

Nakauchi, T. (1976). *Theories of academic ability and evaluation* [Gakuryoku to hyouka no riron]. Tokyo: Kokudosha.

National Institute for Educational Policy Research. (Ed). (2015). *Basic Research on Curriculum Organization Report No. 7: Overview of "principle of curriculum organization towards comprehensive development of competencies"*, (http://www.nier.go.jp/English/departments/menu_8.html#Research).

Nishioka, K. (2009). Issues surrounding academic achievement in Japan: Examining the 2008 revisions of the National Courses of Study. In Japanese Educational Research Association (Ed). *Educational Studies in Japan*, Tokyo: Japanese Educational Research Association, No. 3, pp. 5–16.

Nishioka, K. (Ed). (2008). *Guaranteeing academic ability using 'understanding by design'* [Gyakumuki sekkei de tashika na gakuryoku wo hoshou suru]. Tokyo: Meiji Tosho.

Rychen, D. S., & Salganik, L. H. (Eds). (2003). *Key competencies for a successful life and a well-functioning society.* Cambridge, MA: Hogrefe & Huber.

Saeki, Y. (1982). *Academic ability and thinking* [Gakuryoku to shikou]. Tokyo: Daiichi Hoki.

Sakamoto, T. (1976). *Children's academic and other abilities* [Kodomo no nouryoku to gakuryoku]. Tokyo: Aoki Shoten.

Sanuki, H. (2009). *Academic ability and neoliberalism* [Gakuryoku to shinjiyuushugi]. Tokyo: Otsuki Shoten.

Sato, M. (1997). Cutting through the 'academic ability' illusion: Academic ability is a currency [Gakuryoku gensou wo kiru – gakuryoku ha kahei de aru]. *Hito*, Vol. 25, No. 2, pp. 1–7.

Sato, M. (2001). *Questioning academic ability* [Gakuryoku wo toinaosu]. Tokyo: Iwanami Shoten.

Shimizu, K. (Ed). (2009). *Exploring 'schools with ability'* [Chikara no aru gakkou]. Osaka: Osaka University Press.

Takeuchi, T. (1993). Why problematize learning now? [Ima naze gakushuu wo mondai ni suru noka]. *Educational Studies in Japan* [Kyouikugaku kenkyuu], Vol. 60, No. 3, pp. 1–8.

Tanaka, K. (2003). The question of 'academic ability': Answers based on the postwar history of academic ability and evaluation [Gakuryoku to iu toi – gakuryoku to hyouka no sengoshi kara no outou]. *Educational Studies in Japan* [Kyouikugaku kenkyuu], Vol. 70, No. 4, pp. 3–30.

Tanaka, K. (2008). *Evaluating Education* [Kyouiku hyouka]. Tokyo: Iwanami Shoten.

Tanaka, Y. (2005). Academic ability from the philosophy of 'weakness': From 'strength' focused academic ability to 'weakness' literacy [Yowasa no tetsugaku kara kataru gakuryoku – tsuyosa no gakuryoku kara yowasa no riterashii he]. In Y. Kudomi and T. Tanaka (Eds). *Academic ability creating hope* [Kibou wo tumugu gakuryoku]. Tokyo: Akashi Shoten, pp. 248–73.

Trilling, B., & Fadel, C. (2009). *21st century skills: Learning for life in our times.* San Francisco: Jossey-Bass.

# Part 2

# Instruction

Chapter 5

# Historical overview
# of lesson study

*Terumasa Ishii*

## Introduction

Recently, the Japanese 'lesson study', a method of in-school teacher training in which teachers learn from each other through conferences before, after, or during lesson presentations, has been recognised not only in the United States, but also throughout the world with the publication of J. W. Stigler and J. Hiebert's (1999) *The Teaching Gap* (Hashimoto, Tsubota, & Ikeda, 2003; Lewis & Akita, 2008). Since the establishment of the modern Japanese school system, teachers in Japan have conducted studies examining their own approaches to education by maintaining written records of educational practices, voluntarily establishing educational groups and research organisations, and by organising lesson studies wherein instructors review lessons as a group. This culture, in which teachers learn freely from one another, has contributed to the outstanding quality of Japanese education.

Lesson studies have garnered significant attention in recent years; however, they are merely one component of teachers' studies, and there are various approaches to in-school teacher training in Japan. Most importantly, teachers in Japan have published numerous records of educational practices that describe events and interactions with specific children in classrooms from a first-person perspective in a narrative style. These records have enabled teachers to share concrete examples of exceptional educational practices, in addition to thoughts and insights to support such practices. In order to identify factors that have been instrumental in contributing to the high quality of Japanese education, it is important not to simply imitate lesson studies in form, but to learn from the contents of educational practices that are unique to Japan by examining practical records. Moreover, it is important to be aware of the complex lineage of the Japanese lesson study.

This chapter provides an overview of the history and characteristics of post-World War II Japanese educational practices, in addition to a history of lesson studies specifically, including a discussion of its contemporary challenges. In doing so, this chapter demonstrates how some forms of the Japanese lesson study (i.e., the design-oriented, efficiency-dominant lesson study and the interpretation-oriented, creativity-dominant lesson study) are being implemented in other countries. This chapter also discusses the existence of educational practices and lesson studies of different origins and the need to re-evaluate them (Ishii, 2006).

# I The historical development of the Japanese lesson study and teaching practices

## I–I The historical origins of the Japanese lesson study

The historical origins of the Japanese lesson study date back to the early Meiji era, with the launch of an elementary school based on the 1872 Education Code. M. M. Scott, an American educator, was subsequently invited to Japan in order to introduce and propagate the Western-influenced whole-class method of lecturing. Model instructional methods were then developed in the normal schools and the schools attached to them, and attempts were later made to spread these methods from Tokyo to all other regions. Initially, this was accomplished by distributing publications and through lecturer classes concerning new teaching methods. However, to assist instructors in mastering these methods in practice, teacher training was conducted; this involved the creation of detailed lesson plans, the presentation of research lessons, and lesson evaluation meetings that included observations.

This training method based on the observation and evaluation of lessons was established in the 1890s at all Japanese schools in tandem with the spread of the Herbartian tiered teaching method (Inagaki, 1995). Lesson studies that focus on developing, introducing and disseminating specific models of teaching tend to emphasise the study of lesson plans in advance, followed by the discussion of techniques and lesson methods during post-lesson conferences. Even today, this technique-oriented form of lesson study is implemented in public research meetings at many schools and remains in the daily consciousness of Japanese teachers. Furthermore, it is one point of origin for the modern Japanese lesson study. It should be noted, however, that the form of lesson study highlighted by Stigler and Hiebert is based on in-school teacher training performed by educational administrators, and therefore shares a common lineage with this techniques-oriented lesson study.

The push to reconsider lesson study focused on the development and dissemination of the lesson methods surfaced with the appearance of the Free Education Movement during the Taisho era. Teachers of the Ikebukuro Jidou no Mura Elementary School, who aimed to establish a child-centred 'liberal' education, pioneered the aforementioned narrative-style records of educational practices, which were modelled after Japanese I-Novels (Asai, 2008). Rather than lesson methods, these records of educational practices utilised the live classroom experiences of teachers and children, and hence enabled teachers to discover themselves as educators who had educational missions and rolls beyond national intent while referring to children by their proper names. Furthermore, these records substantiated the act of teachers conveying their personal, practical experiences in their own words and signified the birth of teachers as research practitioners.

This tradition, wherein teachers performed autonomous practical research, became dormant during the 1930s with the approach of World War II and the implementation of Imperial National Training Education. It was revived, however, following World War II and the emergence of democratic education; this, in turn, led to the production of numerous practical records. This was particularly apparent during the early post-war period, wherein a torrent of notable records of educational practices were published successively by teachers partaking in life writing, beginning with Seikyo Muchaku's *Yamabiko gakko* (School Echoing in the Mountains) (1951) and Kenjiro Konishi's *Gakkyuu kakumei* (Classroom Revolution) (1955). Most of the practical records published during this period focused on children's writings (namely essays) and the life skill training surrounding them. In contrast, the practical records of Kihaku Saito and Shima Elementary School teachers (e.g., *Mirai ni tsunagaru gakuryoku* [Academic Achievements that Lead to the Future] [1958]) recount the classroom experiences of instructors and students and demonstrate the potential of conducting classes based on facts extracted from actual practices.

According to Saito (1964), structure of teaching is characterised by a series of tense relationships between children, instructional materials and the teacher. For example, a tense relationship exists between the essence of instructional materials and a teacher's interpretation of them. Tense relationships also arise between teachers and children in interactions during the teaching process. Likewise, tension exists between a child's knowledge and skill level and the requirements of instructional materials. Moreover, tense relationships develop as children exchange opinions amongst themselves. When these relationships become manifest in desirable forms, both teachers and children are capable of discovering and producing something new, and students can obtain a depth of thinking otherwise unattainable through individual learning. Hence, Saito likens the classroom instruction to a drama, wherein children, instructional materials and teachers are performers. Saito's theory and practice was an ideal conceptualisation of the post-war Japanese classroom instruction: a creative whole-class teaching in which the thinking of children is collectively orchestrated by means of an instructor's artful skill. This produced a teacher culture wherein excellence in the art of teaching was emphasised in the form of a so-called 'jugyo-dou'.

Beginning in the late 1950s, organised lesson studies and research on teaching by university researchers were developed (e.g., Zenkoku Jugyou Kenkyu Kyogikai (the Council for Nationwide Lesson Study) in 1963 and Kyojugaku Kenkyu no Kai (the Didactic Studies Association) in 1973), which were led and inspired by Saito's creative educational practices. Therefore, a generalisation of the principles of an exceptional teaching (i.e., the creation of didactics) was proposed through the creation and analysis of lesson records (National Association for the Study of Educational Methods, 2009). With the goal of promoting didactics in mind, researcher-performed lesson studies seek to determine what to teach and how it should be taught based on excellent classroom practices, in addition to research conducted by non-government education research organisations concerning subject content and instructional materials, which was mentioned in Chapter 2 (Shibata, 1967; Sugiyama, 1984).

Researchers, along with teachers, have re-examined existing subject content and instructional materials and have also debated its relevance and relationship to understanding subject content, even during the reorganisation of communication processes in lessons. Furthermore, a considerable number of researchers regard the essence of teaching to be a human art form and emphasise the creative skill required of teachers in designing educational activities, rather than discrete and mechanical lesson techniques. Thus, some theoretical frameworks have been developed that clarify points regarding practical judgements and considerations, which are consistent with the internal processes employed by instructors in their teaching practices (Yoshimoto, 1983; Fujioka, 1989). These differ from describing the construction of a teaching process from the outside (i.e., extracting the type and stage of lesson development that will become the analysis framework for classroom activities and the development and propagation of a corresponding class or lesson method).

### 1–2  The development of various post-World War II teaching practices

This section summarises the historical development of post-World War II teaching practices in Japan in light of representative practical records from each period (Tanaka, 2005, 2009). In the new era of education that followed World War II, empiricism, child-centred approach and life unit learning prevailed in classrooms nationwide. For example, the Japanese language teacher Hama Omura used clippings from newspapers and magazines as learning materials in classrooms that lacked desks, chairs, textbooks, or blackboards; it was against this backdrop that she developed the unit method of teaching, wherein children learn by their own initiative. In her book entitled *Oshieru toyuu koto* (What Teaching Is) (1973), Omura describes the essence of teaching and the role of an instructor based on her own practical experiences. As mentioned earlier, there was newfound interest in life writing during this period, in addition to the spread of practices intended to unify life and education. For example, Yoshio Toi, a well-regarded contemporary of Saito, penned *Mura wo sodateru gakuryoku* (Academic Abilities to Develop a Village) (1957), which is based on life writing and descriptions of creative lessons derived from 'productive failure', the naïve thinking and misconceptions of children in their daily lives. Furthermore, as national control over education strengthened in the 1950s, Saito attempted to demonstrate the potential of teaching as a profession, in addition to the creative nature of conducting a class based on authentic descriptions of classrooms (cf. *Jugyou Nyumon* [Introduction to Teaching] [1960]).

In the 1960s, criticism of the child-centred approach arose, and national courses of study came to be 'announced' to have legal binding force. Various non-government education research organisations (e.g., the Association of Mathematical Instruction, the Hypothesis-Verification-Through Experimentation Learning System Research Group, and the History Educationalist Conference of Japan) attempted to integrate science and education and proceeded to develop plans for the creation of unique subject content and instructional materials (i.e., the modernisation of subject content). Kazuaki Shoji in his book entitled *Kasetsu jikken jugyou to ninshiki no riron* (Hypothesis-Verification-Through Experimentation Learning System and the Theory of Recognition) (1976) proposed an approach to science education based on the Hypothesis-Verification-Through Experimentation Learning System. This instructional method was originally proposed by Kiyonobu Itakura in the 1960s and emphasises experiments that meaningfully convey fundamental scientific concepts, principles and rules (e.g., students may be asked to determine whether steel wool will become heavier or lighter upon being burnt). Hence, investigations such as these begin with the presentation of a problem, followed by a prediction, an argument and then an experiment.

Seiki Suzuki's *Kawaguchikou kara gaikou e* (From the Kawaguchi Harbour to the Harbour Abroad) (1978) proposed the use of tangible objects during social studies lessons in order to promote the understanding of social scientific concepts and laws that cannot be physically observed. On the other hand, in 1958, pioneers in Japanese social studies such as Kaoru Ueda and Takayasu Shigematsu began to criticise moral education and the teaching of systemism, and consequently spearheaded the Syoshinokai (the Society for Achieving the Original Spirit of Social Studies), which entails the cultivation of proactive and independent individuals who are capable of bearing the responsibilities of a democratic society. This is embodied in the lesson studies published by Toyama City's Horikawa Elementary School in 1959, which provide valuable insight into the promotion of independent thinking among children.

With the emergence of meritocracy in the 1970s, the problem of school dropouts became apparent. Accordingly, Hiroshi Kishimoto's *Mieru Gakuryoku, Mienai Gakuryoku* (Tangible and Intangible Academic Ability) (1981) highlighted the need to account for a student's lifestyle and the cultural environment in his or her home, while also proposing methods to establish basic academic skills, such as *hyaku masu keisan* (hundred-square calculations). Likewise, Nakamoto Masao's *Gakuryoku e no chousen* (Striving for Academic Achievement) (1979) provided practical examples of how to teach differential and integral calculus to students at bottom-tier schools in an enjoyable manner through the creation of relevant instructional materials and the utilisation of appropriate tools, such as by teaching mathematical functions using a 'black box'.

Throughout the 1970s and 1980s, the Association of Mathematical Instruction and the Hypothesis-Verification-Through Experimentation Learning System Research Group sought to create 'enjoyable lessons', thereby leading to a re-evaluation of instructional materials and subject content from the perspective of children's independence and the logic of real life. In *Kodomo ga ugoku shakaika* (Social Studies Made by Children) (1982), Toshio Yasui proposed a practice wherein students reflect on historical events in a manner whereby the problems associated with a particular occurrence become their own, thus leading to an empathetic understanding of the viewpoints held by various historical parties and, most importantly, people. Likewise, in his book entitled *Omatsuri eigo gakushuu nyuumon* (An Introduction to Festival English Learning) (2007), Shigemitsu Ahara maintained that English language learning should entail not only the acquisition of basic communicative skills, but also the study of language that facilitates communication with others using each of the five senses. Likewise, in *Rika no toutatsumokuhyou to kyouzaikousei* (Science Attainment Targets and Instructional Material Construction) (1990), Yasutaro Tamada asserted that science lessons should promote the attainment of targets; Tamada proposed a learning task method designed to guide students toward natural and correct awareness by means of experiments and debates centred around learning tasks.

In the mid-1980s, increased attention was placed on teaching skills such as questioning, directing and blackboard use among instructors who were fearful of potential classroom failures and prone to anxiety during the planning of daily lessons. Yoichi Mukoyama's *Tobibako ha daredemo tobaserareru* (1982), which introduced the technique of encouraging a child to leap over a vaulting horse, was the starting point for a movement toward the development of teaching skills based on the sharing and identification of hidden skills in everyday practices. Furthermore, Kazumasa Arita's *Kodomo no ikiru shakaika jugyou no souzou* (Creating Social Studies Lessons That Children Live) (1982) introduced a social studies teaching practice based on the use of instructional materials that children are capable of earnestly investigating. Hisako Tsukiji, a teacher at Andou Elementary School in Shizuoka City (which was a representative practice school for the Syoshinokai), wrote *Ikiruchikara wo tsukeru jugyou* (Classes That Instil a Zest for Living) (1991). In it, she argued that lessons should encourage lively debate and deep inquiry among children; to achieve this, Hisako suggested that teachers should evaluate and steer the thinking processes of children according to individual learning records and seating charts.

As the movement toward an 'escape from learning' progressed during the 1990s, lessons were created with an emphasis on re-examining the meaning of in-school learning and asserted that children should be the central focus of education. Kazuko Otsu's *Shakaika: Ippon no banana kara* (Social Studies: From a Single Banana) (1987) includes classroom records pertaining to modern society that begin with familiar subjects (e.g., a banana), which are then expanded upon to address topics related to developmental and global education. Kimiaki Kato's *Wakuwaku ronsou! kangaeru nipponshi jugyou* (Japanese History Lessons for Exciting Debates) (1991) features lessons wherein high school students are asked to form hypotheses as real historians in order to examine and debate Japanese historical mysteries.

Takayuki Kodera's *Chikyuu wo sukue! Suugaku tanteidan* (Save the Earth! Math Detectives) (1996) consists of math lessons that require students to use their knowledge of mathematical functions to solve problems related to environmental issues, such as waste disposal and the effect of Freon gas on the ozone layer. Moreover, Kazuko Yoshida's *Feminism kyouiku jissen no souzou* (Creating Feminist Educational Practices) (1997) describes home economics lessons that require students to set and investigate learning tasks based on their lived experiences, which can then be linked to modern societal issues.

Toshiro Kanamori's *Sei no jugyou, shi no jugyou* (Lessons on Sex [or Life] and Lessons on Death) (1996) contains 'life learning' accounts from elementary school classrooms; the focus of these lessons is to convey the realities of life and death to children. Also, Hiroshi Imaizumi's *Manabi no hakken yomigaeru gakkou* (Schools That Revive the Discovery of Learning) (2001) discusses teaching practices that promote a classroom atmosphere in which students can speak freely, wherein their mistakes are positively supported. Indeed, the traditions of life education and life writing continue to thrive in these practices.

Integrated studies were adopted in the 1998 National Course of Study, and a specified period was allotted to them. Following this, Wako Elementary School (a Core Curriculum Association's experimental school emphasising life education) released a three-volume series entitled *Wako shougakkou no sougou gekushuu* (Integrated Studies from Wako Elementary School) (2000). Similarly, Mitsuo Otaki, Toshihiko Koda and Kenji Morozumi published *Sodatetaine, konna gakuryoku: Wako gakuen no ikkan kyouiku* (Academic Abilities You Want to Foster: Wako School's Comprehensive Education Programme) (2009). Hajime Obata's *Soko ga shiritai 'kodomo ga tsunagaru' gakushuushidou: naze 'nara joshidaigaku fuzoku shougakkou no ko' no gakushuu ha fukamarunoka* (What We Want to Know About Child-led Educational Guidance: Why Learning among Children at the Elementary School Attached to Nara Women's University Has Improved) (2007) summarises educational practices at traditional child-centred schools since the beginning of the Free Education Movement during the Taisho era.

Shinichiro Hori's *Kinokuni kodomo no mura: watashi no shougakkouzukuri* (Kinokuni Children's Village: How I Built an Elementary School) (1994) describes educational practices that are intended to assist in establishing a liberal/free school similar to A. S. Neill's Summerhill School. *Tomo ni manabi, Tomo ni ikiru 1, 2* (Learn Together, Live Together) (2012) was released by Ina Elementary School and highlights practices from long-term, child-centred integrated studies wherein children learn from life experiences, such as by raising pigs until they are ready to be processed for meat. Moreover, Toshiaki Ose and Manabu Sato's *Gakkou wo kaeru: Hamanogo Shougakkou no gonenkan* (Changing the School: Five Years at Hamanogo Elementary School) (2003) addressed the essence of school reform and discussed the authors' efforts to promote a community of learning.

Therefore, by using practical records to summarise the processes involved in facing and overcoming challenges, Japanese teachers have compiled accounts of creative educational practices, while also becoming the subjects of their own practical research.

## 2 Contemporary issues in lesson study in Japan

### 2–1 The paradigm shift theory of lesson study in the 1990s

Since the 2000s, in-school teacher training focused around open classes has been conducted in various schools in Japan as schools face the demand to improve academic achievement, which necessitates lesson improvement. Furthermore, as the issues related to schools become more complex and trust in teachers and schools wavers, attention is being increasingly drawn to the significance of lesson study that lies at the core of a teachers' learning community (i.e., a place where teachers increase each other's abilities, share and accumulate knowledge and create solidarity), not just from the standpoint of developing each individual teacher's ability but also to increase the school's organisational capacity (Kitagami, Kihara, & Sano, 2010).

However, in a situation where the PDCA cycle pervades educational settings, there is a concern that by being incorporated into the PDCA cycle as a measure to effectively attain improvements in classrooms and schools, the value of lesson study conducted as practical research for teachers may be lost. With the examination of teaching plans, there is concern that such plans may be trivialised as items are filled in accordance with standard teaching plans developed by each municipality. Meanwhile, it is also feared that the post-classroom conference will be reduced to tracing the forms of classroom reflections and improvement plan proposals in accordance with the PDCA cycle.

By the 1990s, Manabu Sato's lesson study paradigm shift theory had been put forward as a theory that could combat the movement of lesson study toward institutionalisation and loss of substance (Sato, 1997). While referencing the two opposing concepts of 'technical expert' and 'reflective practitioner' proposed by D. A. Schön, Sato indicated that the lesson study developed by university researchers from the 1960s onward pursued technical rationality and that lessons were reduced to fit the application range of theories that had been attained (i.e., didactics and science of lessons). As a result, this propelled the formalisation of educational practice and in-school training.

Sato's criticisms were not only addressed toward 'theory into practice' (the lesson study that targets logical application of scientific technologies developed in university laboratories, as practiced in a segment of educational technology research); rather, they were also directed at 'theory through practice' (the lesson study that aims to construct theories based on facts from practices by entering classrooms). Such practice was exercised by the Council for Nationwide Lesson Study and the Didactic Studies Association. Thereafter, Sato advocated lesson study as an activity for re-constructing 'theory in practice' through reflection by placing the teacher's practical research at the centre (Table 5.1).

At the time, the act of teachers 'teaching' was perceived negatively due to two factors that were taking place at the time: the proposal of a new view on academic achievement by the Ministry of Education and the introduction of the newest

*Table 5.1* Two lesson study paradigms proposed by Manabu Sato

|  | Analysis of Classroom Activities Focusing on Technical Practices | Research of Classroom Activities Focusing on Reflective Practices |
|---|---|---|
| Goal | Develop and assess program General recognition that transcends context | Form practical epistemology based on educational experience Awareness specific to certain context |
| Objects | Diverse range of lessons | One specific lesson |
| Basis | Didactics, psychology, behavioral science, positivist philosophy | Social sciences/humanities, practical epistemology post-positivist philosophy |
| Method | Quantitative research, generalization sampling method, nomothetic method | Qualitative research, specification case study method, idiographic method |
| Characteristics | Elucidates cause and effect (causality) | Elucidates meaning of experience and its relation (connections) |
| Outcomes | Development of teaching techniques and materials | Reflective thinking and practical discernment |
| Expression | Paradigmatic mode of knowing | Narrative mode of knowing |

Source: Chart created based on Sato and Inagaki, 1996, p. 121

psychology of learning to emerge since the cognitive revolution. Thus, it was also an era that was shifting toward emphasising active and collaborative lessons that respect children's 'learning'. Sato was at the helm of such a learning-centred approach under the keyword of the learning community. This is how the frameworks of technical experts and reflective practitioners were proposed in Japan by connecting them to the paradigm shift of lesson study, which transitioned from *teaching* to *learning*. Thus, a trend of emphasising ex post facto reflection (reflection-on-action) rather than prior design, and understanding the process of *learning*, rather than examining the act of *teaching*, during the ex post facto reflection was created. On the other hand, emphasising the act of teaching and designing lessons was deemed prone to promptly incite streamlining and inflexibility of educational practice and drill teaching (Figure 5.1).

Most schools' in-school training commonly exhibits a trend where a great deal of effort is expended in prior preparation, with the ex post facto conference becoming formularised or turning into a session of critiquing teaching skills. In contrast, the lesson study proposed by Sato and others places the manner in which children learned in the classroom at the centre of discussion, promoting the enhancement of the ex post facto conference by relativizing the complex events during the lesson. In addition, they set lesson study in the direction of preparing teachers' practical research from the sidelines. Such studies included research on the teachers' practical thoughts and learning process, development

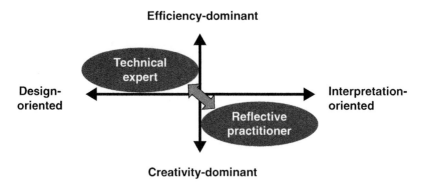

*Figure 5.1* Dichotomous oppositional scheme of technical experts and reflective practitioners in Japan

Source: Created by the author

of classroom reflection tools, and the re-evaluation of narrative practical records (Asada, Ikuta, & Fujioka, 1998; Fujiwara, Endo, & Matsuzaki, 2006). Furthermore, it should be noted that when Japanese lesson study is discussed, particularly in Asian countries, child-focused lesson study as proposed by Sato or school reform concepts for the learning community are frequently referenced.

## 2–2 Re-examination of a dichotomous oppositional scheme of technical expert and reflective practitioner

As a clue for re-examining the dichotomous oppositional scheme between technical expert and reflective practitioner proposed by Sato, this section will highlight the existence of two patterns related to expertise and reflection, respectively (Ishii, 2013).

Expertise research in psychology (i.e., research on the process by which one becomes an expert in a certain field by attaining technical knowledge and skills) proposes the two opposing concepts of routine expert and adaptive expert (Hatano & Inagaki, 1983). A routine expert (efficient expert) refers to those who can apply procedural knowledge that has a pre-determined form ('if this . . . then do this') faster and more accurately. For example, although initially finding it difficult to cook according to a recipe, the learner eventually becomes skilled at cooking as they repeat the same procedure several times. The skills earned through this process are only effective for a specific task and under specific conditions. In contrast, an adaptive expert refers to a state in which one can flexibly re-combine procedural knowledge, expand it and discover new procedures in accordance with the situation.

In the 2005 report *Preparing Teachers for a Changing World* submitted by the U.S. National Academy of Education as a summary of findings related to the knowledge base that teachers should know as well as teachers' learning, such adaptive experts who can make flexible use of the knowledge base to resolve uncertain problems are presented as an ideal image of the teacher that should be aspired to (Darling-Hammond & Bransford, 2005). Furthermore, a study on the knowledge base of teachers, Shulman (1987) points out the importance of the process of adapting knowledge related to the content of school subjects based on the context of educational practice, as well as that of pedagogical content knowledge (PCK), which is formed as a result of the process. The report by the National Academy of Education also emphasises this point. PCK can be said to function within the judgement process of teachers' design process and elucidate the essence of knowledge that bridges theory and practice.

Meanwhile, the dual concepts of single-loop learning and double-loop learning have been proposed for the reflective practice in organisational learning theory. In the 1970s, C. Argyris and Schön (1974) differentiated between the states of organisational learning as single-loop learning, which solves problems based on existing frameworks, and double-loop learning, which is a transformative activity that reconsiders even the appropriateness of the original problem settings (i.e., the existing framework and values). Argyris uses a thermostat as an analogy to illustrate the difference between the two learning states. If the temperature is too high or too low, a thermostat detects this and adjusts to the temperature that had been set; this is single-loop learning. On the other hand, double-loop learning involves reviewing the operating programme and basic policies themselves by also questioning whether or not the set temperature itself is suitable, as well as the precondition value of whether to prioritise comfort or energy conservation. In addition, the reflective practice, accompanied by the reframing of the framework proposed by Schön, presupposed double-loop learning.

## Conclusion

As has been discussed up to this point, the framework of technical experts and reflective practitioners in Japan was proposed by linking to the transition of classroom practice from teaching to learning. As a result, a trend was born in which the reflective practice emphasised the ex post facto reflection rather than prior designing, with the ex post facto reflection unilaterally stressing understanding of the learning process, rather than examination of the act of teaching.

However, the ex post facto conference that performs reflection tends to focus only on describing and interpreting children's unique learning from beginning to end. It is also prone to lacking the viewpoint of examining children's learning in relation to the teacher's instruction and curriculum. In addition, it is rare for the conference to overcome superficial factual exchanges and extend to the deciphering of their significance and theoretical construction (i.e., the organisation of tacit knowledge into formal knowledge).

On the other hand, emphasising the technical process of lessons and the act of teaching was viewed as likely to invite streamlining and rigidity of drill teaching into educational practice. As a result, the technical expert model that provides the foundations of the teacher training programme held by the Japanese government or municipalities remains unchallenged as to whether it has any propensity to reduce to solely learning how-to and skills, lacking an understanding of the contents that are to be taught. This becomes an underlying factor to generate practices that simply follow procedures without deliberating on their meaning.

As indicated in Figure 5.2, the emphasis on becoming technical experts does not immediately signify an emphasis on efficiency. On the other hand, it is necessary to conduct reflection as a problem-exploration cycle spanning up to knowledge creation that re-questions the original framework of problem-setting. Otherwise, it will lead to strengthening only the existing framework, causing rigidity of practices. Furthermore, the creative qualities of experts (i.e., the flexible ability to respond and judge per the situation) that the concept of the reflective practitioner tried to relativise is not something that necessarily opposes the act of designing practices, learning the theory constructed externally to practice and the course of learning that applies these to practice.

The dichotomous oppositional scheme of technical experts and reflective practitioners in Japan, as indicated in Figure 5.1, is prone to overlook the creative thought process developed intentionally for the design of practice before and during the practice. However, this is something that had already been considered in Schön's idea of 'reflection in action'; as such, there is no need to raise J.F. Herbar's educational tact concept.

In the current state where the Japanese dichotomous oppositional scheme of technical experts and reflective practitioners is operating to propel the formulisation

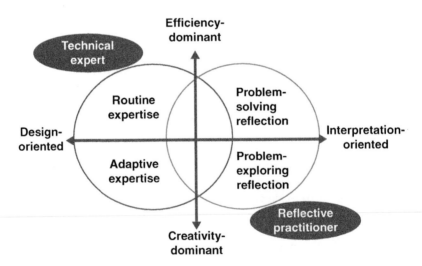

*Figure 5.2* Re-construction of dichotomous oppositional scheme of technical expert and reflective practitioner

Source: Created by the author

of lesson studies, to re-evaluate the other lineage of Japanese lesson studies (i.e., design orientation and creativity-dominance) is becoming necessary (Ishii, 2014). This is particularly so in the present Japan, where there is an increasing number of young teachers who have issues with subject matter studies and teaching practice as a result of massive retirement and the new employment of teaching staff. The study of lessons that exist within the course of teaching and learning is not something that is resolved solely through researching teaching skills, or, conversely, only through research studies on children and learning. The realities of classes that include children's learning research need to be examined in relation to the teacher's intentional prompting (i.e., subjects, materials and methods to be taught). Furthermore, the teacher's internal judgement/consideration process before and during the classes, or, the world of meanings experienced between children, teaching material and teachers needs to be relativised. Thereafter, by focusing on lesson study that aims to create lessons that are not centred on either techniques or children but exist as art will enable contact with viewpoints that perceive classes as dramas and craftsmanship, which has refined lesson study in Japan.

## References

Ahara. S. (2007). *An Introduction to Festival English Learning*. [Omatsurieigogakush-uunyuumon]. Tokyo: Sanyusyasyuppan.

Argyris, C., & Schön, D. A. (1974). *Theory in practice*. San Francisco: Jossey-Bass.

Arita, K. (1982). *Creating Social Studies Lessons That Children Live* [Kodomo no ikirushakaikajugyou no souzou]. Tokyo: Meijitosyo.

Asada, T., Ikuta, T., & Fujioka, K. (1998). *Growing teachers: An invitation to teacher effectiveness training* [Seicho suru kyoshi: Kyoushigaku e no izanai]. Tokyo: Kanako Shobo.

Asai, S. (2008). *Teachers' narratives and new education* [Kyoushi no katari to shin-kyouiku]. Tokyo: Tokyo University Press.

Darling-Hammond, L., & Bransford, J. (Eds.). (2005). *Preparing teachers for a changing world: What teachers should learn and be able to do*. San Francisco: Jossey-Bass.

Fujioka, N. (1989). *Ideas for creating lessons* [Jyugyou zukuri no hassou]. Tokyo: Nihon Shoseki.

Fujiwara, A., Endo, E., & Matsuzaki, M. (2006). *Life history approach toward practical knowledge of Japanese language teachers: Case example studies practiced by Eiko Endo* [Kokugoka kyoushi no jissenteki chishiki he no raifu hisutorii apuroochi: Endou eiko jissen no jirei kenkyuu]. Tokyo: Keisui-sha.

Hashimoto, Y., Tsubota, K., & Ikeda, T. (2003). *Lesson study: Why are we currently researching classes?* [Lesson Study/Ima, naze jyugyou kenkyuu ka]. Tokyo: Toyokan Publishing.

Hatano, G., & Inagaki, K. (1983). Culture and cognition: Concerning the transmission and composition of knowledge [Bunka to ninchi: Chishiki no dentou to kousei wo megutte]. In T. Sakamoto (Ed.). *Contemporary basic psychology 7: Cognition, knowledge, and language* [Gendai kiso shinrigaku 7: Shikou, chinou, gengo]. Tokyo: Tokyo University Press, pp. 191–210.

Hori, S. (1994). *Kinokuni Children's Village: How I Built an Elementary School.* [Kinokunikodomo no mura: watashi no shougakkouzukuri]. Tokyo: Buronzusinsya.

Imaizumi, H. (2001). *Schools That Revive the Discovery of Learning.* [Manabi no hakkenyomigaerugakkou]. Tokyo: Shinnihonsyuppan.

Inagaki, T. (1995). *Study on the history of Meiji-era teaching theories* [Meiji kyoujyu riron shi kenkyuu]. Tokyo: Hyoronsha.

Ishii, T. (2006). The uniqueness and issues of project TK lesson study methodology: Response from the post-war lesson study history [Purojekuto TK no jyugyou kenkyu houhou ron no dokujisei to kadai: Sengo jyugyou kenkyuu shi kara no outou]. In K. Tanaka (Ed.). *Lesson study conducted through collaboration between Takakura Elementary School and Kyoto University Graduate School* [Takakura shougakkou to kyouto daigaku daigakuin tono renkei ni yoru jyugyou kenkyuu]. Kyoto: Grants-in-Aid for Scientific Research Interim Report, pp. 15–38.

Ishii, T. (2013). How to conceptualise the image of teachers as profession: Surpassing the dichotomous oppositional scheme of technical experts and reflective practitioners [Kyoushi no senmonshoku-zou wo dou kousou suruka: Gijyutsuteki jyukurensha to shousatsu-teki jiseenka no nikou tairitsu zushiki wo koete]. In *The exploration of educational methods* [Kyouiku houhou no tankyuu], vol. 16, pp. 9–16.

Ishii, T. (2014). Re-examining lesson studies: Re-evaluation of didactic interest [Jyugyou kenkyuu wo toi naosu: kyoujyugaku-teki kanshin no sai-hyouka]. In The National Association for the Study of Educational Methods (Ed.). *Education method 42, lesson study and in-school teacher training* [Kyouiku houhou 43: Jyugyou kenkyuu to kounai kenshuu]. Tokyo: Tosho Bunka, pp. 36–49.

Kanamori, T. (1996). *Lessons on Sex [or Life] and Lessons on Death.* [Sei no jugyou, shi no jugyou]. Tokyo: Kyoikushiryosyuppankai.

Kato, K. (1991). *Japanese History Lessons for Exciting Debates.* [Wakuwaku ronsou! kangaeru nipponshi jugyou]. Tokyo: Chirekisya.

Kishimoto, H. (1981). *Tangible and Intangible Academic Ability.* [MieruGakuryoku, MienaiGakuryoku] Tokyo: Otsukisyoten.

Kitagami, M., Kihara, T., & Sano, K. (Eds.). (2010). *Designs for School Improvement and In-School Training* [Gakkou kaizen to kounai kenshuu no sekkei]. Tokyo: Gakubun-sha.

Kodera, T. (1996). *Save the Earth! Math Detectives.* [Chikyuu wo sukue! Suugakutanteidan]. Tokyo: Kokudosya.

Konishi, K. (1955). *Classroom Revolution.* [Gakkyu kakumei]. Tokyo: Makishoten.

Lewis, C. C., & Akita, K. (Eds.). (2008). *Lesson study, the learning by teachers: Invitation to lesson studies* [Jyugyou no kenkyuu, kyoushi no gakushuu: Ressun sutadi e no izanai]. Tokyo: Akashi Shoten.

Muchaku, S.(1951). *School Echoing in the Mountains.* [Yamabiko Gakko]. Tokyo: Seidosha.

Mukoyama. Y. (1982). *Everyone Can Make It Possible That Every Child Can Leap Over a Vaulting Horse,* [Tobibako ha daredemotobaserareru] Tokyo: Meijitosyosyuppan.

Nakamoto, M. (1979). *Striving for Academic Achievement.* [Gakuryoku e no chousen]. Tokyo: Junposya.

The National Association for the Study of Educational Methods. (Ed.). (2009). *Lesson study in Japan (Volumes 1 & 2)* [Nihon no jyugyou kenkyuu (jyou/ge kan)]. Tokyo: Gakubunsha.

Obata, H. (2007). *What we Want to Know About Child-led Educational Guidance: Why Learning Among Children at the Elementary School Attached to Nara Women's University has Improved.* [Sokogashiritai 'kodomogatsunagaru' gakushuushidou: naze 'narajoshidaigakufuzokushougakkou no ko' no gakushuu ha fukamarunoka]. Osaka: Osakasyoten.

Omura, H. (1973). *What Teaching Is.* [Oshierutoyuukoto]. Tokyo: Kyoubunnsya.

Ose, T., Sato, M. (2003). *Changing the School: Five Years at Hamanogo Elementary School.* [Gakkou wo kaeru: HamanogoShougakkou no gonenkan]. Tokyo: Syogakkan.

Otaki, M., Koda, T., Morozumi, K. (2009). *Academic Abilities You Want to Foster: Wako School's Comprehensive Education Program.* [Sodatetainekonnagakuryoku: Wako gakuen no ikkankyouiku]. Tokyo: Otsukisyoten.

Otsu, K. (1987). *Social Studies: From a Single Banana.* [Shakaika: Ippon no banana kara]. Tokyo: Kokudosya.

Saito, K., Shima Elementary School teachers. (1958). *Academic Achievements that Lead to the Future* [Mirai ni tunagaru gakuryoku]. Tokyo: Mugisyobo.

Saito, K. (1960). *Introduction to Teaching* [Jugyou Nyumon]. Tokyo: Kokudosya.

Saito, K. (1964). *The development of lessons* [Jyugyou no tenkai]. Tokyo: Kokudosha.

Sato, M. (1997). Opening the Pandora's box: Criticism on lesson study ["Pandora no hako" wo hiraku: "Jyugyou kenkyuu" hihan]. In Sato, M. *Aporia known as teachers: Toward a reflective practice* [Kyoushi to iu aporia: Hanseiteki jissen he]. Tokyo: Seori Shobo, pp. 25–56.

Sato, M., & Inagaki, T. (1996). *An introduction to lesson study* [Jyugyou Kenkyuu Nyuumon]. Tokyo: Iwanami Shoten.

Shibata, Y. (1967). *Contemporary didactics* [Gendai no kyoujyugaku]. Tokyo: Meiji Tosho.

Shoji, K. (1976). *Hypothesis-Verification-Through Experimentation Learning System and the Theory of Recognition.* [Kasetsujikkenjugyou to ninshiki no riron] Tokyo: Kokudosya.

Shulman, L. (1987). Knowledge and teaching: Foundation of the new reform. *Harvard Educational Review, 57*(1), pp. 1–23.

Stigler, J. W., & Hiebert, J. (1999). *The teaching gap: Best ideas from the world's teachers for improving education in the classroom.* New York: Free Press.

Sugiyama, A. (1984). *The creation of lessons* [Jyugyou no souzou]. Tokyo: Buraku Problems Research Institute.

Suzuki, S. (1978). *From the Kawaguchi Harbour to the Harbour Abroad.* [Kawaguchikoukaragaikou e]. Tokyo: Kusadobunka.

Tamada, T. (1990). *Science Attainment Targets and Instructional Material Construction* [Rika no toutatsumokuhyou to kyouzaikousei]. Tokyo: Azuminosyobou.

Tanaka, K. (Ed.). (2005). *Teachers who have pioneered an era* [Jidai wo hiraita kyoushi tachi]. Tokyo: Nippon Hyojun.

Tanaka, K. (Ed.). (2009). *Teachers who have pioneered an era II* [Jidai wo hiraita kyoushi tachi II]. Tokyo: Nippon Hyojun.

Toi, Y. (1957). *Mura wo sodaterugakuryoku* (Academic Abilities to Develop a Village), Tokyo; Meijitosyo.

Tsukiji, H. (1991). *Classes That Instil a Zest for Living.* [Ikiruchikara wo tsukerujugyou]. Tokyo: Reimeisyobo.

Wako Elementary School. (2000). *Integrated Studies from Wako Elementary School* [Wako shougakkou no sougougekushuu] Tokyo: Minsyusya.

Yasui, T. (1982). *Social Studies Made by Children* [Kodomogaugokushakaika]. Tokyo: Chirekisya.

Yoshimoto, H. (1983). *The imagination of teaching* [Jyugyou no kousou ryoku]. Tokyo: Meiji Tosho.

Yoshida, K. (1997). *Creating Feminist Educational Practices* [Feminism kyouikujissen nosouzou]. Tokyo: Aokisyoten.

# Chapter 6

# Practices of leading educators

## Yoshio Toi, Kihaku Saito, Kazuaki Shoji and Yasutaro Tamada

*Koji Tanaka*

## Introduction

This chapter focuses on the four excellent educators (Yoshio Toi, Kihaku Saito, Kazuaki Shoji and Yasutaro Tamada), who sought linkages between life and education and linkages between science and education, and introduces their practices.

## I Yoshio Toi and his stumble analysis

Yoshio Toi (1912–1991) was a teacher committed to real-life writing. After the war, he remained silent for a while as he assumed his own degree of responsibility for the war with deep regret. But when the wave of high economic growth surged even to the mountain village up in northern Hyogo Prefecture, he decided to publish *Academic Abilities to Develop a Village* (Toi, 1957) out of necessity. He struggled with the situation where his students studied hard under his passionate guidance and then left the village for higher education or work. He suffered anguish over the thought that what he was doing was educating them to leave the village.

Toi insisted on education for the purpose of developing a village, but that did not mean to guide children who can live only in a village. What Toi meant was to cherish the region and culture of their own, and educate children who can think rationally and reach out and take the hands of others. Such conflict Toi felt shares the same concept with the agony of teachers and schools of today, who are suffering from questions over the pros and cons of education for entrance exams. This question leads to the issue of achieving education to live and work that Toi has been claiming.

Among many quotes he left, there is no other word than "children are the genius of stumbling" that condensed the means to achieve the education to live and work that Toi pursued (Toi, 1967). It is inconvenient for teachers when their students stumble over something during class, and the teachers wish to avoid such cases, if possible. In contrast, Toi believes that children are geniuses since they do not just stumble over any reason, but they stumble based on a certain rule. This rule stems from the difference between the teacher's logic of curriculum and the logic of real life, which is peculiar to children. Toi insisted that an analysis of such stumbling shall lead to the discovery of a treasury of good guidance.

His perception of stumbling from a totally new angle, his analysis of such stumbling to expose the difference between the logic of curriculum and the logic of real life, and his endeavors to improve the ways of teaching and studying – these were generated from the struggles he fought during his teaching days. It is no exaggeration to say that the above perceptions are the essence of formative assessment, which has been established as the heart of the study in educational evaluations. To put it another way, Toi has been pointing out from early on that formative assessment is not just to check children's academic growth but to improve teaching skills by analyzing their stumbling (Toi, 1958).

Based on his perspectives, Toi was harshly critical of relative evaluations. He said "I give out a heavy sigh every time the end of the term comes. The pen I hold in my hand makes little progress as I try to write report cards. Finally I close my eyes and write down 2. Then, I let out a sigh again . . . 'This child worked so hard, and yet I have to write in 2 again.' 'I kept praising this educationally subnormal boy for his ability to express himself, and yet all he gets is 1' . . . On the last day of the term, after I have given out report cards, I always feel my face stiffen." And so he embarked on educational evaluation reforms when he was a principal (*Reformation of Report Cards*, Meijitosho, 1967). He adopted a three-level absolute evaluation system and valued each child's approach to studying as the attitude toward learning. This is the origin of today's system of evaluations based on targets (Toi, 1967).

## 2 Kihaku Saito and his research on open-ended questions

Kihaku Saito (1911–1981) was practicing as a teacher under the influence of the liberal education that began in the Taisho era. In 1952, he was assigned as a principal of Shima Elementary School in Gunma Prefecture and began his study of teaching and learning. His research is described in his books, and *Academic Achievements that Leads to the Future* (Saito, 1958) and *Introduction to Teaching* (Kokudosha, 1960) played an important role in providing the basis for the research in educational methods. There he writes enthusiastically and demands that teachers be earnest in class.

To explain this in greater detail, he believed that a school should be a place where educators teach children the rich cultures through classes. Obviously, he did not think teaching in classes would solve all problems. But unless the basic function of school is positioned to teach rich cultures in classes, he insisted that all problems surrounding children would never be solved.

Second, he claimed that classes should proceed not by one-way explanations and interpretations by teachers but in a tense relationship between teachers and children as if it is a serious match. To that end, teachers are required to make ceaseless efforts to deepen their knowledge and skills.

Third, his words contain deep political implications. By its very nature, teaching children in classes and raising their academic achievements enables the school to win the hearts and minds of parents and local people, as well as to clarify the power of unreasonable people who try to distort such achievements. He believed that study of teaching and learning is by no means practiced inside a tube.

Among many of Saito's fruitful research studies of teaching and learning, his research on open-ended questions was one of the best. Open-ended questions and closed-ended questions are two different types of questions. Open-ended questions are asked by teachers who know (or think they know) the answer of children who do not know (or think they do not know) the answer. The role of this open-ended question is to activate children's thinking and to confirm their level of understanding. In performance assessments, which came to attract much attention recently, teachers are to develop effective performance assessment tasks to urge children to think and evaluate their understanding. It may be said that open-ended questions play exactly the same role as performance assessment tasks. Above all, asking the "stir-up questions" proposed by Saito requires high teaching skills because the process is aimed at assessing the level of children's acquired knowledge and then destroying their knowledge to obtain a new level of understanding.

Saito was also critical of relative evaluations. He thought relative evaluations were focused only on ranking children and failed to capture their actual situations. He proposed "xx's type of mistake" system, which is also one of Saito's ideas that made him famous. When a child makes a mistake during class, he did not pin the blame on that child, but called the mistake "xx's type of mistake," and classified the same type of mistakes into patterns so that the whole class could share and learn from them. Here, there is a similarity regarding reverse thinking between Toi's perception of *stumbling* and Saito's perception of a *mistake*. Also, from today's point of view, his idea of practicing formative assessments with a group of children was highly innovative.

## 3 Kazuaki Shoji and his cue words

It was 1963 when Kazuaki Shoji (1929–), who was teaching at Seijo Gakuen Elementary School, met Kiyonobu Itakura of the National Institute for Education and proposed Hypothesis-Verification-Through Experimentation Learning System (Shoji, 1965). Before this encounter, he was very much interested in details pertaining to local village customs, as represented in Kunio Yanagida's philosophies on native folkloristic (called "Joumin") and proverbs. Thus, he showed huge interest in the relationship between scientific knowledge and real-life knowledge in children's recognition formation (Shoji, 1976).

Hypothesis-Verification-Through Experimentation Learning System is to precede class through the course of *issue – predict – discuss – experiment* and to manage an enjoyable class. He emphasised that enjoyable classes stem from the criticism of comprehensible classes. The latter has the image of passive lessons where learning takes place simply by using one's brain, while the former has the image of active lessons where learning takes place collectively through the five senses. By this, he meant to warn that scientific education, under the names of "science" and "education," was merely letting children "know" the facts.

Shoji's recognition theory, which will later be summarised as the Theory on Three-Staged Recognition and their Mutual Commitment, is also known as Up and Down Recognition (refer to "Aspects of Recognition"). According to Shoji, to understand things deeply is a state of being capable of going up and down between the first stage, which represents real-life knowledge, and the third stage, which represents scientific knowledge, with the second stage in-between. For example, to be able to explain actual events with scientific theory (to "go down") and to be able to develop scientific theory from the events experienced in life (to "go up") is to really understand things.

*Aspects of Recognition*

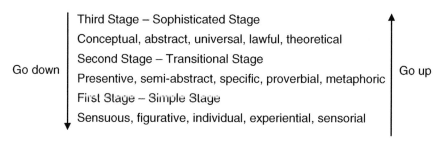

In this regard, to confirm how much this type of understanding is formed in children, he focused on cue words, or in other words, conjunctions. In the reports or during discussions, when such a conjunction as "for example" is used, the state of recognition is *going down*. In contrast, when such a conjunction as "that is" is used, the state of recognition is *going up*. By confirming how and how much these cue words are used, the aspect of understanding of the child can be assessed. Thus, it may be safe to assume that cue words are the rubrics that measure understanding.

On the other hand, Shoji emphasised the importance of self-evaluation in educational evaluations. According to Shoji, "education is to let children maintain their self-awareness, which has gotten better," and for that "teachers need to find ways for children to evaluate themselves." And so he proposed many interesting methods for self-evaluation (explanation method through a virtual technique, manga-drawing method, thread-pulling method, etc.). It is regrettable that such methods cannot be introduced due to space constraints, but there is so much to learn from them as an evaluation method in terms of performance assessment.

I have chosen three educators from the post-World War II age and explained their achievements in the study of teaching and learning. What is common among them is their humanism and realism toward children's growth and progress.

That is apparent in their positive approach to *stumbles* and *mistakes* and in their approach to the structure of children's recognition. Again, I would like to stress that what they brought was not a relic of the past but highly suggestive studies for educational evaluation research.

## 4 Yasutaro Tamada and his objectives-based approach

On the other hand, from the perspective seeking the linkage between science and education, studies of subject matter that deepen the equality between the content of school subjects and attainment targets have often been conducted. Yasutaro Tamada (1927–2002), a representative man of practice in the Association of Science Education, was an outstanding teacher who elaborated a variety of teaching methods based on the studies of the content of school subjects. Tamada clarified the attainment targets, selected the effective instructional materials and developed the teaching practice called the learning task method based on the objectives-based approach (Editorial Committee of "Introduction to Teaching Practice in Science" (editing and writing), 2008).

### 4–1 Clarification of attainment targets

As the attainment targets are specified and set up as teaching targets (aims and purposes), the teaching practice in which the aspect of class is different from the one based on the progressive targets becomes possible. The first thing to note is that teachers can check their teaching practice based on the aims as the targets are clarified, and the purposes lead to the encouragement of children in their studies. Of course, there is no need to announce today's purpose at the beginning of each class (although this is a commonly used method of teaching), but it is important that teachers and children commonly recognise what type of academic achievement can be made in the class. On the other hand, if only vague effort targets are given as progressive targets, it is difficult for teachers to clearly sense children's changes that occurred in the class (and for children to clarify what they learned and what they could not understand).

### 4–2 Attainment targets and instructional materials/ teaching processes

The next thing is that clarification of target enables a variety of ideas and elaborations in the educational method to help children achieve the target. For example, suitable instructional materials and tools can be selected or created, and appropriate teacher questions and explanations can be elaborated, depending on the nature and point of children's difficulty. In other words, by clarifying the target, it becomes clear that the setting of attainment targets and the creation of instructional materials/teaching processes are actions at different levels in teaching theory; therefore, a variety of instructional materials/teaching processes can be elaborated in order to achieve the attainment targets; however, instructional materials/teaching processes are basically regulated by the quality of attainment targets to be set. If setting of attainment targets and creation of instructional materials/teaching processes are separated and only the latter is taken care of, that action is criticised as "technicism."

Yasutaro Tamada's practice aims at lessening the basic and essential attainment targets and creating a wide variety of instructional materials. For example, in order to achieve the attainment target that gas occupies space and has mass, a variety of materials are used, such as air, carbon dioxide, nitrogen, oxygen and butane, as instructional materials. Let's clarify the teaching flow to explain the fact that *gas also has mass*. First, a teacher clarifies how the weight of the whole gas bottle changes if air is put in the bottle using a bicycle pump, then the instructor proceeds with such comments as "weigh a liter of air," "weigh a liter of this gas and consider whether it is air (carbon dioxide is used)," and "how can we confirm that the gas is carbon dioxide or anything else (nitrogen is used)."

### 4–3 Attainment targets and cooperation/individualisation of instruction

Furthermore, by presenting common attainment targets to children, cooperation of instruction becomes possible and the conditions are met to organise a learning group and to encourage cooperative competition. Needless to say, children are involved in an exclusive competition and always exposed to the stress of a highly competitive educational system, which has become an international issue (concluding observations of the Committee on the Rights of the Child, United Nations 1998), under the circumstances where progressive targets and relative assessment are prevailing. Neither teachers nor parents are free from the exclusive competition either. However, the attainment targets should not be kept in secret by teachers but should first be opened to children in order to surely organise a learning group by setting common attainment targets. In addition, a contract securing the attainment targets for children needs to be executed between the teacher and children with the parents involved. An instruction valuing the attainment targets by openness and contract is given a power of motion to promote children's cooperative activities.

With regard to this point, how should the individualisation of instruction be understood? First, the *individualisation of objectives* and the *individualisation of instruction* should be differentiated. The individualisation of objectives means a way of thinking to set each objective, depending on a differential of children's academic achievement. However, the attainment target theory that is in a position of securing the right to learn and academic achievement is critical of the individualisation of objectives that presupposes and further increases a risk of, a differential of academic achievement. On the other hand, the individualisation of instruction is to individually approach children who have stumbled in the learning process and to give guidance depending on the nature and condition of each child's stumble when common attainment targets are set. Of course, the cooperation/individualisation of instruction can flexibly be used based on the children's participation in the class and the condition of their stumble.

In Yasutaro Tamada's practice, a one-hour class proceeds as follows:

(1) The teacher presents a learning task.
(2) Children write 'their opinions' in their notebooks.
(3) The teacher confirms the distribution of children's ideas to conflicting ones by a show of hands.
(4) Children present their opinions and discuss.
(5) Children write what they think after hearing others' opinions in their notebooks.
(6) The teacher confirms the distribution of children's changed ideas after the discussion by a show of hands.
(7) The teacher (or children in some cases) confirms the hypothesis by experiment.
(8) Children write the experiment results and what they have learned in their notebooks.
(9) The teacher has children read the experiment results and what they have learned, starting with a child who has finished writing.

It can be understood that the individualisation of instruction is realised in the learning task by making children's cooperative learning a basic principle and by consciously incorporating the task of writing in a notebook.

For example, based on the attainment target that for plants, flowers are the organs for reproduction, the teacher first has children observe the structure of flowers and the mechanism of pollination using rape plants as the instructional material and then presents to the children the question as to whether the fruits and seeds will be produced after tulip flowers bloom. As an advanced learning task (1), which initiates a discussion. Of course, many children think that tulips are grown from bulbs and they do not produce fruits or seeds from their past life experience and adjacent learning experience (2, 3). On the other hand, some think that tulips produce fruits and seeds, and then, a presentation of opinions and a discussion by children starts (4). After that, one of the children wrote, "What I think after hearing others' opinions" (5), which reads as follows. "First, we heard an opinion that tulips would produce seeds because they were plants. I opposed to the opinion. The reason is that I have never heard of tulip seeds and we plant tulip bulbs. I'm against that opinion. Next, we heard a strong opinion that tulips are grown from bulbs. I'm for it. Then, someone asked why there are stamens and pistils." It is imaginable how the children's discussion went on (6).

Then, children have come to understand that tulips produce fruits and seeds with surprise by being instructed to observe the ovaries and ovules of tulip pistils and to gather fruits and seeds as well (7). Therefore, one of the children wrote "the experiment results and what I have learned" in the notebook as follows

(8, 9). "There was an ovule. I saw what grew afterwards. Ripe seeds were in purplish red, thin and triangle-shaped. From this observation, it is certain that tulips produce seeds. I have learned even bulbous plants bloom and produce fruits and seeds. Uchida asked why bulbs are planted instead of seeds. I think the reason is that it takes longer till flowers bloom if seeds are planted. That is why bulbs are planted." From this notebook, it can be understood that children face the learning task, actively discuss and those listening to the discussion also fully participate in the cooperative learning.

### 4–4 Attainment targets and formative assessment

Attainment Targets have raised an important perspective in a teaching practice. Specifically, they differentiate the assessment functions into diagnostic assessment, formative assessment and summative assessment and especially focus on the role of formative assessment. Formative assessment is conducted in the teaching process, where conventionally, teachers who were skillful in teaching practice elaborated various teaching techniques (teacher question, class monitoring, notebook check and quiz, etc.) to check children's responses in the class, which were taken out as formative assessment, and the teachers tried to share them as common property of all teachers. Then, the teachers immediately modified their teaching practices based on the obtained results and children checked their learning activities based on the feedback. In this way, realism is being pursued in the educational practice by showing to what extent children have actually achieved the attainment targets for the items the teachers mistakenly thought or believed they have taught.

Formative assessment was raised in order to share the skilled teachers' essence as a common property, and it is not necessary to limit the interpretation to just giving quizzes. As mentioned above, Yoshio Toi said, "Children are the genius of stumbling" and tried to probe into the "logic of subject matter" and the "logic of everyday life." Kihaku Saito raised the sharing system of errors and shared difficulties. These actions are valuable assets in the formative assessment theory in our country. In Yasutaro Tamada's practice, the role of formative assessment is mainly assumed by notebook guidance.

Furthermore, the target of formative assessment should not be beyond what was taught, and the results should immediately be reported to children together with (open) criteria. In that case, the teacher should carefully explain why and where they made a mistake so that they do not focus only on scores. Then, the teacher conducts the corrective activities for children who stumble based on the results of formative assessment. On the other hand, when most of the children in the class have achieved the basic academic ability, the teacher organises the enrichment activities (for example, to make questions for friends, to teach friends and to write a report, etc.) and through this process, the development of academic ability such as elaboration of knowing and reorganizing their understanding is secured.

This chapter has described the characteristics of plentiful assets in the lesson study in Japan. The most prominent characteristic was the position to secure the educational objectives/contents, which are comprised of the basis/foundation of learning and culture, for all children, and therefore, it was the effort to clarify targets, value children's independent activities by the combination of elaboration of instructional materials and cooperation and individualisation, and in addition, ensure the academic achievement by conducting the formative assessment. The plentiful assets in the lesson study are attracting attention again in the educational environment in modern Japan, where comprehensive learning abilities and active learning are emphasised.

## References

Editorial Committee of "Introduction to Teaching Practice in Science" (editing and writing). (2008). *Introduction to Teaching Practice in Science: Learning from Yasutaro Tamada's Study and Practice Achievement* [Rika no jugyou dukuri nyumon: Tamada Yasutaro no kenkyu, jissen no seika ni manabu]. Tokyo: Nippon hyojun.
Saito, K. (1958). *Academic Achivements that Lead to the Future* [Mirai ni tsunagaru gakuryoku]. Tokyo: Mugishobo.
Saito, K. (1960). *Introduction to Teaching* [Jugyou nyumon] Tokyo: Kokudosha.
Shoji, K. (1965). *Hypothesis-Verification-Through Experimentation Learning System* [Kasetsu jikken jugyou]. Tokyo: Kokudosha.
Shoji, K. (1976). *Hypothesis-Verification-Through Experimentation Learning System and Recognition Theory* [Kasetsu jikken jugyou to ninshiki no riron]. Tokyo: Kisetsusha.
Toi, Y. (1957). *The Academic Abilities to Develop a Village* [Mura wo Sodateru Gakuryoku]. Tokyo: Meijitosho.
Toi, Y. (1958). *Stumble in Learning and Academic Ability* [Gakusyu no tsumazuki to gakuryoku]. Tokyo: Meijitosho.
Toi, Y. (1967). *Reformation of Report Cards* ["Tsushinbo" no kaizou]. Tokyo: Meijitosho.

Chapter 7

# Various methods for organizing creative whole-class teaching

*Terumasa Ishii*

## Introduction

As was mentioned in Chapter 5, creative whole-class teaching that collectively elaborates the thinking of children by means of the teacher's art has formed the core of the vision for teaching in post–World War II Japan. In this chapter, I will demonstrate a methodology for designing such a 'teaching as a drama' approach through a re-evaluation of a lineage of Japanese lesson studies (i.e., design orientation and creativity-dominance), one which was forgotten in the paradigm shift of teaching practices from teaching to learning in the 1990s.

## 1 The traditional image of 'good teaching' in Japan

Many teachers in Japan have pursued teaching that takes full advantage of the meaning of studying in class groups and that pools together the ideas of students and elaborates on them. Various ideas are exchanged and chemical reactions occur between them, and discoveries and knowledge that cannot be generated by individuals alone are produced. Owing to this, it has been attempted to guarantee results for ability formation and growth of learners while enhancing the learning process. For example, the teaching of Kihaku Saito and Yoshio Toi, who are practitioners representing the post-war era, is typical of this type of teaching. Here, I will introduce a summary of the teaching of 'The Burning of the Rice Field', which was conducted among fifth grade (elementary school) students by Toi at the end of the 1950s (Toi, 1987; Kawaji, 2005).

'The Burning of the Rice Field' is a story in which a village headman named Gohee has a premonition that a tsunami will hit his village. In order to save the 400 villagers from the tsunami, he sets fire to the rice fields, which are awaiting the harvest, inducing the villagers to flee to the top of a hill to escape the fire and saving their lives. In reading this work, student A had written in his notebook a reading that differed from the author's intent: for the scene in which Gohee has finished setting fire to all of the rice fields, and then throws away his torch and gazes out at the coast, his reading was that 'Gohee has burned all of the rice plants that had produced a bumper crop, and then is gazing out at the coast while probably thinking to himself that he has done a regrettable thing.' Toi had student A present this reading during group in his class.

When he had done so, the other classmates unanimously muttered 'That's strange!' Accordingly, Toii intentionally posed a question that supported student A: 'So Gohee set fire to the rice that had been harvested with such difficulty, and then probably thought that he done something regrettable, right?' When the teacher said this, the students said, 'If it were us, we would probably think that we had done a regrettable thing, but we think that that is not the case with Gohee.' In response, the teacher asked, 'If so, what is the evidence for that?' With that question, the students eagerly set about finding the evidence.

When they had thought about it for a time, student B let fly the following statement: 'Before Gohee set fire to the rice fields, he said "It is a waste, but I can save the lives of the entire village by doing this." If we read here, we can see that on the one hand Gohee thinks that it is regrettable that he has set the fire. However, the word "but" is added after that, and that is saying the opposite. Here, he is weighing the value of the rice against the lives of the villagers. However, as a result of weighing these against each other, Gohee has been able to decisively state that "the lives of the entire village can be saved by this."' This meaning of Gohee's decisive statement was a point that even Toi had not noticed. In response to this discovery by the students, Toi thanked student A, saying, 'Today we were able to engage in a wonderfully vigorous and valuable study; however, if we consider the reason why, it is because student A shared that reading with us.' The above is an overview of Toi's practice.

In Toi's teaching, the child's 'stumble' (an erroneous response or opinion that diverged from the correct response) was not treated negatively; rather, 'elaboration' was launched with the 'stumble' or 'productive failure' as the starting point. This way of proceeding is meaningful not only for the child who has stumbled but also for other children who think that they know the correct answer. It is common that these children, even when they can express their answer clearly, cannot respond skilfully when pressed about the reasons for their idea. It is possible to achieve a deeper level of understanding by explaining one's own ideas and citing one's evidence to a person who may have a different idea, or teaching a person who has yet to understand the point. Above all else, At the moment when the students' understanding was shaken and they tried to seek an explanation from the text, a sort of internal concentration and a tense atmosphere in a good sense must have emerged, like the climax of a drama, in Toi's classroom, and many students must have felt excitement in which it seemed as though something was going to happen.

## 2 Teaching as a drama and the teacher's art

### 2–1 Teaching as a drama

There is a tendency when discussing 'teaching' to encounter the extreme argument that anyone can handle 'teaching' as long as he or she is familiar with the content to be taught, or as long as there is a manual. In contrast, it may also be claimed that teaching depends on talent and personal magnetism. It is certain at least that teaching demands skill and competence from teachers. Teaching is an occupation in which the tone of the teacher's voice, the way in which he or she makes eye contact, and his or her physical stance and posture all make a statement, and in which the personal maturity of the teacher is also consistently under scrutiny. However, it is possible for anyone to achieve such skilled competence by continuing to learn in a research-type fashion amidst one's daily practice, with a proper methodology ('teaching as the practice of a profession').

Teaching is a process in which 'teacher' and 'children' interact through the medium of 'teaching material', leading cultural content to be acquired and abilities to be gradually formed. That situation can be established by a deliberate approach based on the teacher's sense of purpose, within a curriculum and learning environment organised by educational intent. Yoichi Mukoyama (1985), who led the 'Teacher's Organization of Skill Sharing', cited the following example: 'Is it satisfactory for a doctor whose patient says "I have had a high fever for 3 days" just to express his sympathy by responding, "That must be terrible"? Would you entrust your life to a doctor who said, about a commonplace disease, "I do not understand the cause, and I do not know any method for treating it. In any event, I will try to do my best?"' While citing this example, Mukoyama stated that the teacher's work lies precisely in making it possible for students to do what they could not previously do, and that what is needed is not only 'love' and 'thought' but also concrete 'techniques' that could change children's cognition and behaviour.

However, what deserves attention here is that, 'techniques in education' cannot be implemented mechanically, like a factory, at the convenience of their creator. Every child has his or her own personality, and children teach themselves ceaselessly, improving themselves on the basis of their own desire and effort. Moreover, the occupation of teaching is a creative process in which students interact with each other in complicated ways; learning often goes beyond the teacher's intentions and is deployed in a rhythm of tension and relaxation in the atmosphere ('teaching as drama'). It is precisely because lessons in school are a creative, dramatic process that it is possible to realise comprehensive and meaningful teaching effects, including not only deeper understanding and creative thinking but also rich internal experience.

### 2-2 Practical decisions as the core of a teacher's competency

If we understand teaching as a creative occupation like drama, it becomes clear that it cannot be carried out simply by generalised individual techniques and the application of material or method X. In interactions in which the children, the teacher and the subject matter are interwoven, the teacher makes a decision extemporaneously. The teacher receives the individualistic reactions of the children, reconsiders and recombines his or her techniques to create something new in response, boldly changes the initial plan, or re-sets the objectives of teaching themselves.

The importance of such judgements and careful consideration in the teacher's work has been emphasised in a variety of forms, for instance as 'pedagogical tact' (the ability to respond as the occasion may demand in teaching) and 'dilemma management' (the work of a teacher making split-second decisions from time to time and continuing to make do in response to the innumerable dilemmas that arise in the process of teaching) (Shibata, 1967; Yoshimoto, 1983; Sato, 2010). In daily teaching, which appears plain and unconnected to drama at a glance, a teaching approach is established by the continuation of extemporaneous decisions. As noted by Herbart, educational tact is the minimum requirement but at the same time the maximum requirement for teachers.

The teacher's work is basically characterised by complexity and uncertainty in a way that may differ from other job types that are called professions, such as those of the physician and the lawyer. In those cases, the technical knowledge that serves as the basis for their professional character is clear. However, owing to the comprehensiveness and complexity of the work involved in teaching, it is difficult to clarify such knowledge base when it comes to the teaching profession. For example, educational activities are not effectively organised solely due to the fact that the teacher is well versed in the scholarly content of some specialised subject, or merely because he or she deeply understands the ways in which children learn or the course of child development. The logic of subject matter content does not necessarily match the logic of children's learning, and in order to connect these logics, knowledge related to methods for rearranging scholarly knowledge as educational content while envisaging the needs of students and for organizing and teaching learning activities with an educational intent (didactic knowledge) will be helpful. Moreover, it is necessary for teachers to continue to inquire about the values and goals to be aimed at in teaching and learning. In this manner, insight and judgement integrating specialised knowledge spanning a variety of fields to design and implement teaching and learning processes are the core of the professional competence of a teacher, and the extent of validity of judgements and depth of insight determines the degree of the teacher's expertise.

## 2–3 The teacher's path of learning

How should a teacher's practical skills and judgement be polished? That process basically takes the form of 'learning by doing', as also in the study of skills in areas such as sports and the performing arts. In other words, it is not a matter of studying theory outside the classroom and applying it in practice; rather, the teacher thinks reflectively over the course of practice and continues to self-regulate his or her practice to make it better while accumulating discipline (as a kind of practical knowledge). Therefore, in order to polish a teacher's abilities, the key point is how the entire process of design, implementation and reflection for teaching is to be enhanced in terms of increasing the opportunity for study by teachers themselves.

In addition, such learning by teachers is carried out within multi-layered joint relationships, in vertical, horizontal and diagonal directions, among teachers of the same age and between them and their senior colleagues. For example, the process of learning from senior colleagues (the experts) and creatively imitating them as models is important for inexperienced teachers. 'Imitating' as used here does not mean simply mimicking their actions superficially, but also thinking things like 'What would Teacher So-and-So think about this?' in response to situations before their eyes and sharing their vision of teaching as well as their ways of thinking and feelings (Ikuta and Kitamaura, 2011). The more thoroughly experienced teachers' ways of facing up to problems and objects as practitioners are imitated and implemented, the more likely a younger teacher will be to achieve the confidence and grounding to begin to build his or her own personal style (graduation from the model).

The majority of the practical knowledge needed to support excellent decisions is hard to put into words that are logical and explicit; instead, it is accumulated by practitioners individually and in collaboration as implicit knowledge (sensory and unconscious knowledge), rooted in memories of specific episodes and the feelings and meanings attached to them. This kind of practical knowledge is accumulated in communities of practice and learned on an on-going basis through vicarious as well as direct experiences and the chance to apply one's intuitive judgement and see it mediated by real episodes and examples. Crucial elements of this process are thinking in the manner of admired teachers every day, engaging in dialogue about teaching and students with one's colleagues and reading and writing records of practice.

As teachers acquire implicit practical knowledge through experience in this manner, however, it is also important for them to study various theories (formal knowledge) related to subject matter content, children's learning, educational methods, etc. It is not the case that teachers can come to practice skilfully just by studying theories, but it is a mistake to say as a result that teachers should not study theories. Teachers should become self-aware about theories that support their own practice so that such awareness helps them understand the meaning of practice from a broader perspective and possess the language to describe it. This awareness informs a teacher's sensory decisions and increases their confidence in their judgement and also prepares them to be innovative and flexible in practice. Research studies carried out by teachers themselves should unite theoretical and practical knowledge through imitation and reflection processes (Ishii, 2012). In the following sections, I will present a 'framework for teaching practice' that indicates key decision points for teaching practice and will relate a methodology of practical research by teachers to foster teachers' growth.

## 3  Methodology for polishing teaching skills

### 3–1  Thinking process for designing a class based on the 'framework for teaching practice'

Several problem areas can be found in the steps for teaching children using teaching materials (Fujioka, 1989; Nakauchi, 1998; Fujioka, 2000). Since the validity of responses given by teachers on the key decision points influences whether classes succeed or fail, it is important to learn the general principles on each decision point. The author has organised the key decision points into the "framework for teaching practice" seen in Figure 7.1; decision points in teaching practice are organised into five categories.

First off is the 'Goals and objectives of teaching' (henceforth, 'Goals'). These ask, 'What contents should I teach, what sort of abilities should I foster, what sort of people do I wish my students to become?' It means to carefully select, clarify and structure education goals and education objectives.

Second is 'Teaching materials and learning tasks' ('Tasks'). These ask, 'Through what subject matter and activities shall goals and content be learned?' Once the goals have been established, then teaching materials and learning tasks need to be designed so that what teachers want to teach becomes what children want to learn.

Third is 'The structures of learning arrangement and environment' ('Structures'). These ask, 'On what timeline should the flow of the classroom activities be organised, how should the style of learning, grouping and spacing be designed, and how should the cultural environment for learning be rethought?'

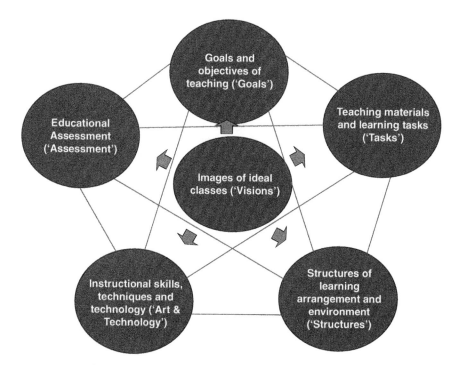

*Figure 7.1* Framework for teaching practice
Source: Created by the author

That is, where should teaching materials and learning tasks be placed within a lesson or a unit? How should the adopted style of learning, grouping and spacing be structured? And furthermore, what sort of community or culture is being created in the classroom? These form the backbone (structure) of classes and learning units and will guide the flow of children's learning activities and thinking.

Fourth is 'Instructional skills, techniques and technology' ('Art & Technology'). These ask, 'How should children be encouraged, verbally and physically? How should technology and media be used?' Even when superior teaching materials and learning tasks are designed, and class formats and spaces are properly structured, if, nevertheless, subjects are presented inefficiently, explanations are hard to understand, unruly behaviour is displayed, and/or information devices are not properly used, then classes will not run smoothly.

Fifth is 'Educational assessment' ('Assessment'). This asks 'By what methods shall learning processes and results be ascertained, and how might those results be used to improve teaching and learning?' No matter how much planning goes into things, children do not necessarily learn as teachers intended. Therefore, it is important to establish means for making learning visible and to attempt improvements for the next day's class, or to adjust one's way of teaching and classroom processes, while identifying any new gaps that arise.

Let us further explain the process of thinking about designing teaching in accordance with the 'framework for teaching practice'. As an example, we will consider a way of teaching the concept of 'insects' in a science class. When asked what insects should be used as examples or subject matter in teaching the concept of 'insects' to elementary school students, many Japanese people might suggest the Japanese rhinoceros beetle, butterflies, dragonflies, ants, cicadas, grasshoppers or spiders as options. When deciding which of these is most appropriate, some people may think that students will be motivated if the popular Japanese rhinoceros beetle is used. What ought to be considered here are the essential details that must be incorporated when introducing the concept of 'insects'. In classes on the concept of 'insects', it is important to introduce the common characteristics of insects (e.g., insect bodies consist of a head, thorax and abdomen, and six legs grow out from the thorax; growth occurs through metamorphosis). If insect body structure is the only important thing, selecting ants is acceptable, but if we want to teach about metamorphosis, butterflies would be considered more appropriate. Moreover, it is easy to raise butterflies, and students may also develop an attachment to and interest in the butterflies through the activity of raising them. Thus, while keeping in mind the achievement of the 'Goal', a 'Task' has been considered that stimulates the interest of students, and through which understanding of target content is deepened.

Then, by thinking about 'Structure', we can design classes that are like drama programmes and that deepen learning and understanding of concepts by instilling in-depth impressions. First, we may introduce the concept of 'insects' using butterflies, which present the typical characteristics of 'insects'. Afterward, we ask, 'Well, are spiders insects?' Now, although spiders are usually thought of as 'insects', biologically they are not. However, the students are now aware of the existence of spiders, and their conceptualisation of 'insects' has become firmer.

Then, students, most of whom seem to understand the concept of 'insects', are introduced to the Japanese rhinoceros beetle, in which is difficult to see the essential characteristics despite its being an 'insect', and they are asked, 'But, is the Japanese rhinoceros beetle an insect?' In this manner, the question will arise among the students: 'Wait, what's going on?' Their understanding will be jolted. Discussion will arise between those students who believe the Japanese rhinoceros beetle is an insect and those who do not, and a spirit of inquiry will be inspired, leading to the further question, 'What are they really?' The students will then observe a real Japanese rhinoceros beetle and discuss whether or not it is an insect; this is a good opportunity to test the student's capabilities to understand the concept of 'insects' and make scientific inferences. In this way, using paired and group learning approaches may be more effective than having the entire class talk together in terms of giving all of them the opportunity to think and communicate. By making sure the students have a grasp of the characteristics of the Japanese rhinoceros beetle, as well as insects in general, we allow them to gain a clear understanding of the concept of 'insects' through an emotional experience that has left a deep impression.

Furthermore, even if 'Tasks' and 'Structures' are designed well, without skilful 'Art & Technology' it will not be possible to achieve the expected dramatic unveiling during class or to reach in-depth understanding. Even if teaching materials are laid out using butterflies, spiders and Japanese rhinoceros beetles and a class structure is designed that can elicit cognitive conflict in each student and intellectual debate among students, without skilful introduction to inquiry it will not be possible to arouse the student's enthusiasm and critical thinking when class proceeds. In addition, if the instructions or rules teachers provide to the students when observing butterflies or Japanese rhinoceros beetles are vague, or the teachers are not able to make skilful use of equipment to conduct observations or present specimens, there is a risk that classes will be chaotic. The teacher's skills in giving instructions in actual practice, non-verbal communication, and ability to improvise according to situation have a significant impact upon the quality of the actual classroom experience.

In many cases, even if a class is held in which a deep understanding of a concept like 'insect' is achieved through emotion, as above, 'Assessments' are made using an objective test to challenge the students' fragmentary knowledge. For instance, pictures of ants can be shown, and the names of the different parts given in response: 'head', 'thorax', 'abdomen', or 'antenna'. However, this results in gaps involving 'enriched classes but poor assessments'. That is, the students adopt a learning strategy involving recall of fragmentary knowledge to be assessed. If a class places importance on the formation of images in the brain and the architecture of knowledge networks, then assessments need to be able to reflect or visualise this. For example, if understanding of the concept of 'insect' is required, then it might be okay if a student is simply shown a picture of an ant with only the head, thorax and abdomen drawn in, and then is made to draw the legs from where they originate. In addition, they might be shown multiple animals and then be asked to identify which are and are not insects and why. In order to achieve enriched, deep learning, consistency (alignment) must be maintained between goals, instruction and assessment.

Furthermore, these five categories do not indicate the steps or procedures that are actually followed; instead, they clarify the details involved, going back and forth. For example, goals may be reset and clarified in the steps devoted to preparing instructional materials and designing assessment methods. Furthermore, as shown in Figure 7.1, judgements made using the five stipulated points and considering the validity of selections are guided by the 'Images of ideal classes' ('Visions') aimed for by teachers. As the image of an ideal class is a disputed issue in education, it is important to always ask yourself what your own image is of the ideal class: *I want to teach children like this, I want to organise a particular classroom group like that, I want this kind of class.* This image should be kept in mind and aimed for daily.

### 3–2 Practical study tools for teacher development through teaching

As already stated, in order to polish their teaching skills, it is important for teachers themselves to pursue practical study through all the steps of class development and implementation: design, implementation and reflection (the 'Cycle of Teacher's Practical Research': Figure 7.2). The direction in which

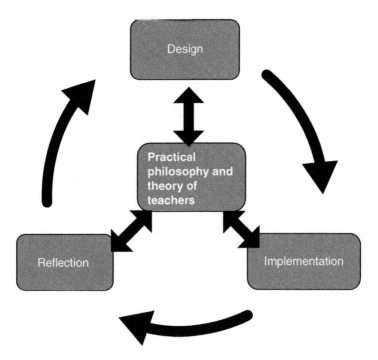

*Figure 7.2* Cycle of teacher's practical research

Source: Created by the author

the practical research cycle develops is guided by the philosophy of the teacher (ideal images of students, classes and schools, and fundamental value etc.). In addition, the validity of judgements made at each phase is governed by 'theory in practice' (consisting of tacit knowledge and explicit knowledge) concerning curriculum content, students, class format and classroom management methods built up by the teacher through theoretical learning and practical experience. At the same time, throughout the design–implementation–reflection cycle of educational activities, teacher philosophies and theories are rethought in practice.

Whether or not the design–implementation–reflection cycle of educational activities becomes the cycle by which a teacher engages in practical research plays a part in whether the refinement or reframing of a teacher's philosophy, theories, or skills (teacher learning and growth) are stimulated. When this does happen, the 'reflection' phase in particular does not merely stop with assessment of student learning in the classroom or means to improve subsequent classes (problem-solving); it is important in addition for goals and assessment validity themselves to be subject to investigation and for there to be discussion that deepens understanding of how educational activities are conceived and executed and the steps by which children learn (knowledge creation). Thus, following a cycle of design–implementation–reflection jointly managed with other people is effective in stimulating knowledge creation. These are aspects of lesson study in Japan that have been getting attention in other countries.

In Japan, in addition to informal learning by individual teachers in their everyday practice, multiple venues for formal learning exist for teachers, as follows: (1) theoretical and methodological/pedagogical lectures and training available through boards of education and universities, (2) independent external study groups such as non-government education research organisations and study circles (where teachers bring records or documents of their regular teaching practice and offer mutual critique), and (3) in-school teacher training focused on lesson study (publicly held classes inside or outside schools offering advance or follow-up conferences). The purpose of (1) is mainly the acquisition of knowledge and skills, whereas the purpose of (2) and (3) is mainly to exchange practical experience, reflect upon it and jointly come up with new/better practical theories and methods.

As stated in Chapter 5, since the 1990s, lesson study has been about stimulating consciousness and rethinking 'theory in practice', which has suggested the importance of post-class case studies. This has gone in two directions, from different starting points: case studies for the study of 'learning' and of 'teaching'.

An example of the former is found in *Class Conference* by Manabu Sato and Tadahiko Inagaki (1996). Especially Sato came to emphasise the importance of pursuing the meaning and connections of learning, in preference to targeting the process of teacher's decision-making in teaching. Furthermore, these leaning-centred approaches advanced the development of reflection tools to support teachers' reflection on past practical experience. An example is the card-constructing method developed by Kanji Fujioka, in which classes are held and observed and as many potential problems or concerns as can be thought of are written on cards, one issue per each card. Then, the cards are stacked and divided into two groups, which are then subdivided into two again. The divided card groups are labelled, and then a structural diagram is created in which label pair connections are indicated by lines, and reasons for them and realisations about the groupings are noted. This encourages classroom instructors to visualise how they see their own classes and to become conscious of a variety of things (that is, it fosters teachers' awareness) (Fujioka, 2000).

Examples of the latter are the 'intervention class' by Kihaku Saito and the 'stop-motion method' by Nobukatsu Fujioka. In the former, a supervising teacher takes over a class from the one normally instructing, asks the children questions and intervenes in the class in response (Saito, 1977). In the latter, reproduction of the video record of a class is temporarily stopped, and a discussion is held on the teacher's teaching method, covering various aspects. The intention is to ask questions on points such as 'Why was this approach taken with this subject?' and 'What were you seeing regarding the children's learning at that time?' and thereby to investigate the intent of the teacher and the process by which they make judgements that inform their activities (Fujioka, 1991).

The case study methods proposed by Inagaki, Sato, or Fujioka etc. were based on amassed practical study by teachers in an attempt to get more benefit out of in-school teacher training and overcome stagnation. For example, Koichi Ito (1990) asserted that the purpose of in-school teacher training was not to achieve a uniform system for schools, but for each teacher to create their own classes and to raise the level of their teaching. Under this assumption, the in-school teacher training proposed by Ito stressed the importance of interpretation of teaching materials and, moreover, in doing so, suggested that 'self-interpretation of teaching materials' by teachers should precede 'interpretation of teaching materials in expectation of [the interpretations of] classes'. Teachers ought not to be treated merely as persons who teach, but as human beings with their own valuable experiences and thoughts. This is compatible with the view that subject matter studies are an opportunity for teachers to grow as learners.

In addition, in lesson plans prepared in Japanese schools, interactions between teachers and students (particularly expectations of student's regarding speech, actions and cognitions in response to teacher encouragement) are described in detail (Figure 7.3). In addition, blackboard plans visualising and organizing such communication and thinking processes are often mentioned. Regarding 'Art & Technology', Japanese teachers have stressed visualisation processes for cultivating thinking in the classroom using blackboards (Figure 7.4). Using blackboards on which lesson material is left after class has concluded, teachers can check the thinking processes of students and the conclusions drawn and properly instruct them to put down their learning and thinking processes in their notebooks, deepening their thinking and causing them to internalise lessons. The use of

Field for writing down students' anticipated thought process for solving tasks.

Field for writing down teacher's guidance and assessment procedure designed to encourage student learning.

Learning task for present session:
"Students prepare diagrams representing the flow of tasks leading up to the installation of the tide protection facility and consider the methods for realizing their goals and ideas."

Teacher's guidance:
"If students do not present their own ideas to the entire class, show them the municipal hall's website and advise them that they can send their proposals directly.
• Prepare cards showing key words, and allow the students to move about as they complete their diagrams.
• Encourage the students to consider balancing their own ideas with those of the public by asking them whether it is really ok that their own wishes alone should prevail."

Anticipation of some students' thought process:
"Rather than focusing exclusively on one's own ideas, one should investigate what the local people think about the situation." → "Taxpayer money will be used, so one should give some consideration to the necessity of the facility before putting forward the proposal."

Some students' problem awareness for next lesson:
"Would everyone in the community be ok with spending taxpayer money on preserving local traditions for future generations?"
The other students' problem awareness for next lesson:
"Traditions should be preserved. A proposal should be prepared and put forward to relevant persons such as councilors."

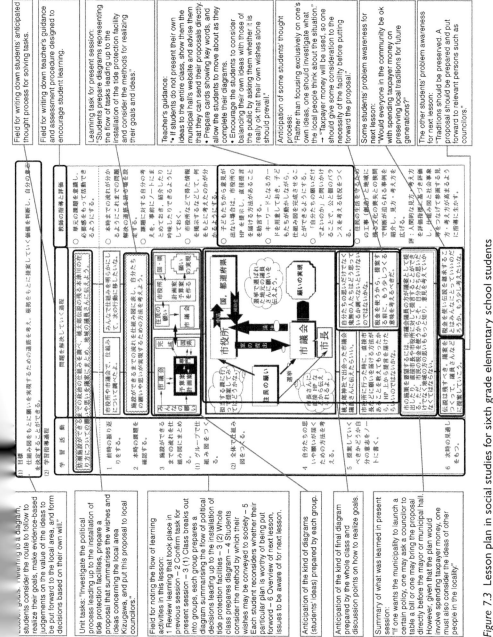

...refering to a diagram, students consider the route to follow to realize their goals, make evidence-based judgements on the value of the ideas to be put forward to the local area, and form decisions based on their own will."

Unit tasks: "Investigate the political process leading up to the installation of tide protection facilities, prepare a proposal that summarises the wishes and ideas concerning the local area Kizugawa, and put this proposal to local councilors."

Field for noting the flow of learning activities in this lesson:
1 Review learning that took place in previous session – 2 Confirm task for present session – 3 (1) Class breaks out into groups, each group prepares a diagram summarising the flow of political decisions leading up to the installation of tide protection facilities – 3 (2) Whole class prepares diagram – 4 Students consider the method by which their wishes may be conveyed to society – 5 Each student reconsiders whether their particular plan is worthy of being put forward – 6 Overview of for next lesson.

Anticipation of the kind of diagrams (students' ideas) prepared by each group.

Anticipation of the kind of final diagram prepared by the whole class and discussion points on how to realize goals.

Summary of what was learned in present session:
"If one wants the municipality to launch a certain policy, one may ask a councilor to table a bill or one may bring the proposal directly before the mayor or municipal hall. However, given that the plan would involve spending taxpayer money, one must also consider the ideas of other people in the locality."

*Figure 7.3* Lesson plan in social studies for sixth grade elementary school students

Source: Prepared by Shoji Kawada, a teacher at Takamatsu Elementary School Attached to department of Education, Kagawa University. The boxes within the figure and the annotations are by this author.

① "Is there a value that can be assigned to x in the equation $x^2 = 10$?": Question posed in present session.

② "If there exists a square whose area is 10 units, then there must also exist a number that can be squared to make 10.": First step in investigating the session question.

③ By thinking in simple terms, the existence of a square whose area is 10 units was confirmed.

④ Having approximated the square root of 10 to seven decimal places, the class focused on Student A's hypothesis that "you can't completely express it in decimals, but you might be able to with a fraction."

⑤ "Can all decimals be expressed as a fraction?" Based on this question, raised by Student A, a question to explore during the next lesson was decided and shared among the whole class.

⑥ A conceptual diagram was drawn up to summarise a matter not yet clarified in the lesson so far (decimals include finite and infinite decimals; infinite decimals include recurring and non-recurring decimals, which can be expressed as fractions). In the following lesson, the concepts of rational numbers and irrational numbers were introduced, and the conceptual diagram was redrawn.

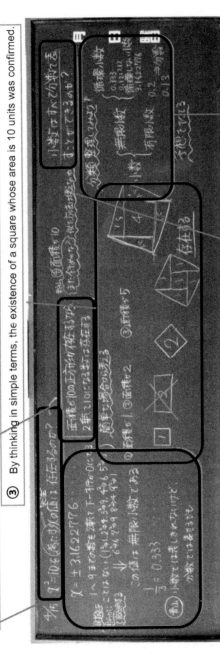

*Figure 7.4* Example of a blackboard in a mathematics lesson for third grade junior high school students

Source: Kazuyuki Kambara, a teacher at Shinonome Junior High School Attached to Hiroshima University. The boxes within the figure and the annotations are by this author.

blackboards and development of techniques for teaching note-taking in Japan clearly reveals the Japanese classroom culture, in which an hour-long class takes on the aspect of a drama programme and emphasis is placed on acquiring knowledge and deepening understanding during each hour of class.

Furthermore, lesson plans in Japan often include mention of the learning and living conditions of certain students (sample students) to whom teachers wish to pay particular attention. In particular, some teachers, sticking with the Syoshinokai, have proceeded by noting details about individual students on seating charts: How is their thinking progressing with regard to the topic of a teaching unit? How is each student in the class expected to think or express themselves? And also, how do they actually think and express themselves (Figure 7.5)? Thus, it is not simply a matter of taking the entire class as a group – each individual student is viewed as rich in their understanding, making for a class that is creative throughout.

## 4  Conclusion

Since the 1990s, there has been an emphasis on case studies for the research of 'learning', and it has been grasped that the careful planning of classes and writing of detailed lesson plans is tied to rigidity and formalisation of classes (Ishii, 2014). Devising and planning classes is not the same as filling-in each field of the lesson plan; it also includes things that are difficult to put into words, and teachers need to imagine specific actions and interactions between students and themselves. Therefore, advanced preparation is not a matter of simply sorting out the form of the lesson plan; one must also ask what the image of the classroom interaction and students learning. Actually, prior to the '90s, formats and methods for advanced discussion of lessons plans were sought to improve the competency of teachers to design classes not to control and standardise classes, but to reflect and develop original processes for designing classes.

A double-loop reflection that might arrive at a rethinking of how teachers view classes, learning and children will not simply arise on its own. Instead, it is important for case studies to become an everyday thing if we are to increase the possibility such reflection can occur. To that end, as promoted by Sato and Inagaki, without putting too much into advanced preparation, it may be effective to create opportunities for discussion in a relaxed environment, for the purpose of interpreting the meaning of students learning and what goes on in the classroom. In addition, in more formal training situations, it may be effective if reflection tools are used, to bring about special opportunities for visualising what one is focusing upon in classroom observations and to notice or become aware of one's own view of classes and education. On the other hand, in order to deepen understanding of curriculum content and improve teaching skills, studies of subject matter, putting energy into advanced preparation, and case studies carefully examining the validity of interventions with students, such as the stop-motion method, are effective. In particular, opportunities to carefully go over precise studies of subject matter

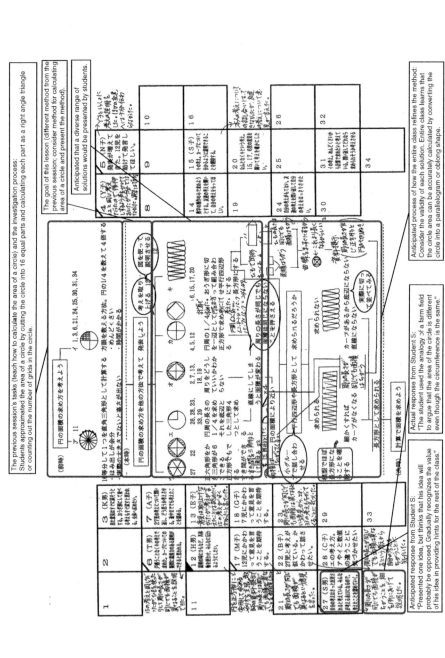

Figure 7.5 Lesson plan with seating chart

Source: Kaoru Ueda, Ando Elementary School in Shizuoka City 1999, Ando Elementary School Presentation: Lesson for Discovering Individuality [Ando shōhatsu ko o mitsumeru jyugyō], Meijitosho Shuppan Corporation, pp. 114–115. The boxes within the figure and

and classroom processes may be important for novice teachers, in order to help them learn how to put together classes, view the students and establish their own teaching styles.

## References

Fujioka, K. (2000). *Intent to involvement* [Kakawaru koto he no ishi]. Tokyo: Kokudosha.

Fujioka, N. (1989). *Ideas for creating lessons* [Jyugyou zukuri no hassou]. Tokyo: Nihon Shoseki.

Fujioka, N. (1991). *Lesson study method through stop-motion method* [Sutoppu moushon houshiki ni yoru jugyou kenkyuu no houhou]. Tokyo: Gakuji Shuppan.

Ikuta, K., & Kitamaura, K. (Eds.). (2011). *Craft language* [Waza gengo]. Tokyo: Keio University Press.

Ishii, T. (2012). In order for regular teachers in regular schools to make their own classes unique [Futsuu no gakkou de futsuu no sensei ga jibun rashii yoi jugyou wo suru tameni]. In *Development* [Hattatsu], 130, Kyoto: Minervashobo, pp. 10–17.

Ishii, T. (2014). Re-examining lesson studies: Re-evaluation of didactic interest [Jyugyou kenkyuu wo toi naosu: kyoujyugaku-teki kanshin no sai-hyouka]. In the National Association for the Study of Educational Methods (Ed.). *Education method 42, lesson study and in-school teacher training* [Kyouiku houhou 43: Jyugyou kenkyuu to kounai kenshuu]. Tokyo: Tosho Bunka, pp. 36–49.

Ito, K. (1990). *In-school teacher training with changing classes with changing teachers* [Kyoushi ga kawaru jugyou ga kawaru kounai kenkyuu]. Tokyo: Kokudosha.

Kawaji, A. (2005). Yoshio Toui and the academic skills to raise a village [Toui Yoshio to mura wo sodateru gakuryoku]. In Tanaka, K. (Ed.). *Teachers who have pioneered an era* [Jidai wo hiraita kyoushi tachi]. Tokyo: Nippon Hyojun, pp. 75–86.

Mukoyama, Y. (1985). *The laws and regulations that improve the classroom* [Jugyou no ude wo ageru housoku]. Tokyo: Meijitosho.

Nakauchi, T. (1998). *Toshio Nakauchi collection I* [Nakauchi Toshio chosakushuu I]. Tokyo: Fujiwara Shoten.

Saito, K. (1977). *Record of an intervention class (top)* [Kainyuujugyo no kiroku (Jou)]. Tokyo: Ikkei Shobo.

Sato, M. (2010). *Educational methods* [Kyouiku no houhou]. Tokyo: Sayusha.

Sato, M., & Inagaki, T. (1996). *An introduction to lesson study* [Jyugyou Kenkyuu Nyuumon]. Tokyo: Iwanami Shoten.

Shibata, Y. (1967). *Contemporary didactics* [Gendai no kyoujyugaku]. Tokyo: Meiji Tosho.

Toi, Y. (1987). *The academic abilities toward the growth of the roots of life* [Inochinekko wo sodateru gakuryoku]. Tokyo: Kokudosha.

Yoshimoto, H. (1983). *The imagination of teaching* [Jyugyou no kousou ryoku]. Tokyo: Meiji Tosho.

# Part 3

# Assessment

# Chapter 8

# Historical overview of assessment in post-war Japan

*Koji Tanaka*

## I Appearance of educational assessment

In my hand, there is the recently reprinted "Research Meeting Records for Teacher Training (2)". These words are recordings of research meetings known as the prehistory of the IFEL (Institute for Educational Leadership) that had been incorporated at the beginning stages of the war. Within, it already introduces the new concept of evaluation that is later translated into Japanese as educational assessment. Furthermore, it considers the "Eight Year Research" of Tyler (Tyler, R.W.) who is an advocate of the concept of evaluation, and small amounts of the enthusiasm for educational reforms at the time can be felt.

Needless to say, the process of understanding the concept of this evaluation did not go so smoothly. In addition, as a typical case that points to the level of understanding of evaluation at the time, created from the battles of translation work such as this, "The Principal of Primary Education" (1951) created by the Ministry of Education can be raised. Within, the features of the concept of evaluation in the early post-war period are explained clearly with the following five points. (1) Evaluation considers the entire lifestyle of the student, and promotes his or her development. (2) Evaluation considers not only the results of the education, but its importance is in the process. (3) In addition to evaluation conducted by the teacher, self-evaluation of the student must also be picked up as an important aspect. (4) Evaluation and its results are also conducted for the selection of more appropriate teaching materials and for the improvement of teaching methods. (5) Evaluation is necessary for effective learning activities.

By reading these regulations, the clear innovation of the post-war educational reforms embedded into educational assessment can be felt. At the same time, starting with such insight, we cannot help wondering why educational assessment became a possession of the teacher and how it became an act of simple checks of the competence of students in the subsequent history.

Next, I would like to think about this point.

## 2 The dual structure of the post-war educational assessment: Relative assessment and intra-individual assessment

The main reason for the educational assessment that began with such deep insight resulting in the act of estimation of students is in the issues of relative assessment of the first post-war cumulative record summary that was adopted, which is evident in the light of subsequent historical facts. So why did relative assessment mix with educational assessment in the early stages of post-war? It is conceivable that there were limits in the translation of the applicable American literature, or there were issues with the translator not being able to make the distinction between measurement and assessment (furthermore, examination and assessment). Or are both of the above the issue? It is an issue where clarification is awaited as historical research.

However, the point to note is that the relative assessment introduced did not play the role of the villain from the start. Rather, it was expected as an aspect to overcome the subjectivity and arbitrariness that existed in the examination pre-war. For example, in the case of examination pre-war, with the subjective judgement of the teacher, the number of students who would receive the grades of Excellent, Satisfactory and Pass was predetermined, and in grading, there was a discrepancy in the number of teachers who would give the grade of Excellent among soft grading teachers and hard grading teachers. This creates a difference in the value of the grade Excellent. However, if the allocation rate of the grade was determined beforehand (5–7%, 4–24%, 3–38%, 2–24%, 1–7%), similar to the Five Level Relative Assessment, then it was believed that objectivity with a sense of fairness and liberation can be secured.

### 2–1 Issues of relative assessment

However, once the educational competition associated with rapid economic growth swept the Japanese islands in the 1960s, relative assessment begins to play its role as the vanguard. Furthermore, this situation led to the spread of the perception of relative assessment being an act of estimation of students more than anything else. With the Report Card Incident (an incident where a letter of objection aimed towards relative assessment was sent to a TV station from a parent of an elementary school student) in 1969, the issues of relative assessment became apparent. Here, I would like to organise the issues of relative assessment that became apparent in these circumstances into three points.

First, it is a non-educational assessment theory that assumes there are students who cannot keep up. For example, in a class of 40 students, a grade of 5 will be given to two to three students. On the other hand, a grade of 1 will also have to be given to two to three students. Here, there flows an underlying way of thinking of Social Darwinism (Survival of the Fittest) that supported the educational measurement activities that flourished in the 1920s saying that there are students who excel, and there are always students who fall behind no matter how you guide them. This is where the heartful teacher is troubled when filling out report cards in the five-level relative assessment, and where they are torn when having have to unreasonably allocate 2s and 1s when everyone in the class gave it their utmost effort as a result of the teacher's guidance. The second issue of relative assessment is that making exclusive competition the norm creates a perception that studying is a win/loss. In a case where the allocation rate of the grade is determined beforehand, someone needs to fail in order for you to receive a higher grade, therefore relative assessment forces an unnatural and exclusive competition, and it forms the mood that the unhappiness of others is the happiness of oneself. Needless to say, here, the competition in general (for example, the competition of emulation in order for everyone to receive 5s) is not being denied, but an exclusive competition is the issue.

The third issue of relative assessment is that it is not an assessment that reflects the actual state of academic achievement. Even if a student receives a 5 in a five-level relative assessment, it means only that the position of the student is high relatively in a group, and it does not prove that the academic achievements earned there reflect the educational objectives aimed for. Rather, it works in inverse proportion to the strengthening of the learning perception of studying as a win/loss, and the question of what was learned will surely become diluted. It can be said that one of the largest issues regarding examination academic abilities lies here.

## 2–2 Role of the intra-individual assessment

By the way, an aspect that cannot be forgotten when speaking about educational assessment theory is that intra-individual assessment along with relative assessment was adopted from the first cumulative guidance record post-war. This was specified into columns of items deemed particularly necessary in educational guidance and the course of guidance overall. This intra-individual assessment adjusts to the line of sight of students and attempts to assess the students comprehensively and developmentally. It is something that came about from the criticisms of examination pre-war that clearly places absolute trust in teachers.

However, once relative assessment is strengthened, it creates a strange dual structure between relative assessment and intra-individual assessment. For students who cannot improve their grades in the Rating column (relative assessment) of the cumulative guidance record, a relationship of relief of the level of effort was created in the Observation column (intra-individual assessment). For example, for a student who received a grade of 3 that was close to 4 in the five-level relative assessment, the number of correct could now be increased in the Observation column.

Although it is a harsh way of looking at it, objectively, this sort of activity was merely a way for the teacher to express his or her sentiment, and it only played the role of kindliness and comfort. This intra-individual assessment allowed for, using terms of sociology, motive adjustment and secondary value; in other words, it added value to the effort that was not being rewarded and began to function as a means for revitalisation. Accordingly, this joint structure of intra-individual assessment that buffers the contradictions of relative assessment continued to strongly regulate the existence of educational assessment post-war.

As shown above, by understanding the structure of the dual structure of post-war educational assessment, one can understand the inner reasons as to why relative assessment maintained the lifeline to today when it was met with many criticisms at first. Intra-individual assessment played the role of alleviating the pain that comes with relative assessment and in the relationship between student and teacher. Furthermore, with this level of understanding, it allows one to look at the possibilities of intra-individual assessment. That is, the issue is not with intra-individual assessment itself, but it was forced to play a miserable role due to its connection with relative assessment. Rather, it has the fascination as an assessment theory. Therefore, in order to rehabilitate the original intra-individual assessment, it is necessary to cut the tie between these joint structures. And to continue the story a little, the combination of objective-referenced assessment and intra-individual assessment is the direction that opens up its possibilities.

## 3 Meaning of objective-referenced assessment

While the issues of relative assessment became apparent, influenced by Bloom (Bloom, B.S.) of the United States, (Ishii, 2011) objective-referenced assessment (called attainment assessment or achievement assessment) emerged in the mid-1970s. To summarise its meaning and give a description, it is as follows.

The meaning of objective-referenced assessment, more than anything else, is that it rehabilitated the role of the original educational assessment. According to Toshio Nakauchi, who is the opinion-leader of attainment assessment, the role of educational assessment is to aim to secure the academic abilities that structure the right to live for the students, for the faculty to self-examine their educational activities, and to function to provide the students with an outlook of their educational activities (Nakauchi, 1971). Needless to repeat, the reason why this educational assessment has been looked upon as an act of estimation of the students is because it is based on relative assessment. In relative assessment, the ability and effort of the student may be questioned unilaterally; however, there is no opportunity to re-question the nature of the education in practice. On the contrary, objective-referenced assessment captures the degree to which the objectives are achieved by students, and if the guidance is insufficient, the educational activities of the teacher can be modified, or support can be provided regarding the educational activities of the students. With this meaning, objective-referenced assessment attempts to pierce through realism with education in practice.

Next, regarding objective-referenced assessment, the facts of the objectives come into question. In this case, there is the National Course of Study as a basis for objectives and content; however, it is not something that is absolute. If we recall the role of educational assessment mentioned earlier, by questioning the education in practice, not only does it question how the class is formed (evaluation of instruction), but it leads to the self-examination of how the curriculum is formed (curriculum assessment), which is structured by objectives and content. Furthermore, through this type of questioning, the cultural content, qualities and abilities necessary to live as sovereigns of public society are set as objectives. And for the students living in the transition stage, the encouragement to live and to enrich them with cultural content, qualities and abilities are also set as objectives.

The categorisation of educational objectives into attainment targets and progressive objectives was proposed by Kiyonobu Itakura (Itakura, 1971), the originator of the Hypothesis-Verification-Through Experimentation Learning System. These two categories are defined as follows.

Attainment targets: The term "attainment targets" indicates targets that require the complete mastery of specific limited knowledge or abilities.

Progressive targets: The term progressive target refers to a target in which having a specific skill is preferable.

Regarding the need to compare the relative differences in how much a person can do (quantitative difference) in order to differentiate between attainment targets and progressive targets, Itakura had the following aims. He thought that the targets at the compulsory education level must be composed of minimum essentials, those things that every child should learn as a citizen of the nation. In contrast, he criticised progressive targets as being naturally inclined to becoming competitive selection tests and being a harmful influence in the classroom.

He also thought that in order to set attainment targets that all children can learn (basic/general concepts and laws of science) as part of compulsory education, it is necessary to create a new educational culture (instructional materials and teaching methods, etc.) in science education. For Itakura, this new educational culture was his proposal of the Hypothesis-Verification-Through Experimentation Learning System based on the lesson plan system. It is important to understand the indivisibility of teaching practices and setting attainment targets.

Itakura's concepts of attainment targets were taken up and developed by Toshio Nakauchi, one of the early proponents of attainment assessment. The most prominent characteristic of attainment assessment was its assertion that, in order to overcome relative assessment, it must recognise the inseparability between attainment theory and assessment theory, requiring a recombination of attainment theory. Nakauchi resolved this relationship, as shown below, using a schema that consisted of progress targets – relative assessment and attainment targets – attainment assessment.

Attainment Targets substantially indicate what the child must acquire, such as "able to solve quadratic functions" or "knows the industrial structure during the Edo Era." In addition, there is a structure and system between those targets and related targets, and it is possible to impart these to the children using instructional materials and tools. The assessment theory that uses these targets as its standard is called "attainment assessment."

Progressive Targets are those that do not have minimum requirements, such as "shows an interest in the wonders of nature" or "develops a willingness to solve problems on his own," and that simply indicate a direction. The assessment theory that uses these targets as it standard is called "relative assessment."

When comparing the two theories of educational objectives and the differentiation of attainment targets and progressive targets, Itakura focused on the quantitative difference (difference in quantity achieved), and Nakauchi focused on the qualitative difference (substance = subject content and function = interest or desire). However, what they held in common was the problem pointed out with progressive targets, which would be, at the compulsory education level, a disincentive for children in acquiring attainment targets made up of the basics of science and culture.

Based on Nakauchi's opinion, he takes a human rights perspective on attainment targets that are set in this manner, saying, "This is an obligation of the government (the community) related to the right to learn (the right to receive an education), which forms the cultural aspect of people's rights as citizens." This "right to learn" emerged in the 1970s as an educational concept in criticism of nationalism and meritocracy and stated that learning is fundamental to the very existence of a child and provides the potential for development. As such, when they do not understand something, children have the right to be taught in a way they can understand. With this view, he claimed that the country's education administration, the educational rights of parents, the research of teachers and the freedom of education should all be bent to the task of protecting the "right to learn" and protecting academic achievement for all children.

Furthermore, the meaning of objective-referenced assessment lies in the encouragement of cooperation among people involved in the assessment activities. Relative assessment creates an exclusive competition among students; in other words, it disseminates the dogma of the survival of the fittest into the education in practice. Needless to say, teachers and guardians are not free from this dogma. On the contrary, with objective-referenced assessment, it allows the organisation of the conditions for students to cooperate/share in achieving an objective, which as a result requires the teachers and guardians (furthermore, people of the region involved in education) to cooperate/share to achieve an objective. In this meaning, objective-referenced assessment brings change to the internal structure of education in practice, and it gives an outlook of the reforms in the systems that support the education in practice.

## 4   New ground level of educational assessment – the combination of objective-referenced assessment and intra-individual assessment

### 4–1 The theoretical constraint of objective-referenced assessment

As shown above, the issues regarding relative assessment are apparent, and with the revisions of the cumulative guidance record in 2001, objective-referenced assessment was finally adopted. This acted as a clear message of assessment theory that supports the securing of academic achievements of students, and its historical meaning is quite clear.

However, from around the time of its appearance before and after, questions and criticisms had been brought up saying that objective-referenced assessment was merely a check of whether the student achieved the objectives the teacher conceived. There were concerns that it encouraged the crushing of objectives and cramming knowledge into students' heads. To clarify in advance, it was not that these issues occurred in all of the classrooms in which objective-referenced assessment was practiced. Furthermore, the countless efforts that have been given to overcome these questions and concerns are also fact.

However, the theoretical constraints that existed that attract these criticisms regarding objective-referenced assessment must be acknowledged. There was this idea of filling in the educational objective (purpose) of the students with the educational objective (aim) raised by the teacher, and it would result in pre-established harmony on both sides without it reaching a certain point. Furthermore, there was the danger that the classes may adopt an approach of compelling pupils' understanding rather than nurturing their understanding.

What became an opportunity to gain strong awareness through this sort of theoretical restraint was the learning model proposed by cognitive psychology that had made remarkable advances during this time. The students were not simply copying the content of what the teacher was instructing, but by comparing the academic and life experiences and through discord (sometimes in the form of rejection or ignoring), they were participating in learning independently and actively. Therefore, in recognizing the contradiction that exists between educational objectives and learning objectives first, and by understanding this contradiction multilaterally and its multilayers, the role of educational assessment becomes the securing of dynamism of the classes. The combination of objective-referenced assessment and intra-individual assessment was something that was asserted with this sort of context by Koji Tanaka (Tanaka, 2008).

By the way, with the National Course of Study revised in 1999 in Japan, integrated study was proposed. And as a form of educational assessment fitting to this integrated study, portfolio assessment was introduced (Nishioka, 2003), and as something to relieve the suppression of the educational assessment thought to be held by the objective-referenced assessment described above, it was welcomed. In Japan, the One Page Portfolio Assessment (OPPA) was developed by Tetsuo Hori.

OPPA is a practice that many teachers follow (see Figures 8.1 and 8.2). It was devised by Tetsuo Hori, who introduced the "naive concept" to Japan (8). OPPA is a method where students record their class achievements before, during and after class on one sheet (OPP sheet: One Page Portfolio Paper) as a learning record, causing students to evaluate themselves. As opposed to a normal portfolio assessment, the point is to maximise the least amount of information necessary for assessment, because it uses one sheet of paper (Hori, 2003).

It allows teachers to review the learning progress before, during and after the lesson, as well as organise and prepare what students record on the sheet of paper

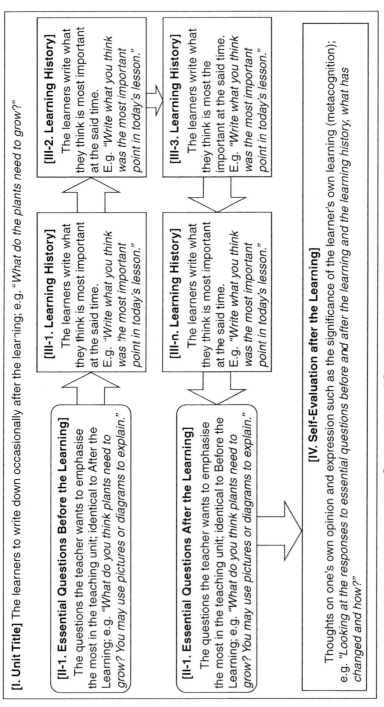

Figure 8.1 Components and overview of the OPP sheet

Source: Hori, 2011, p. 53

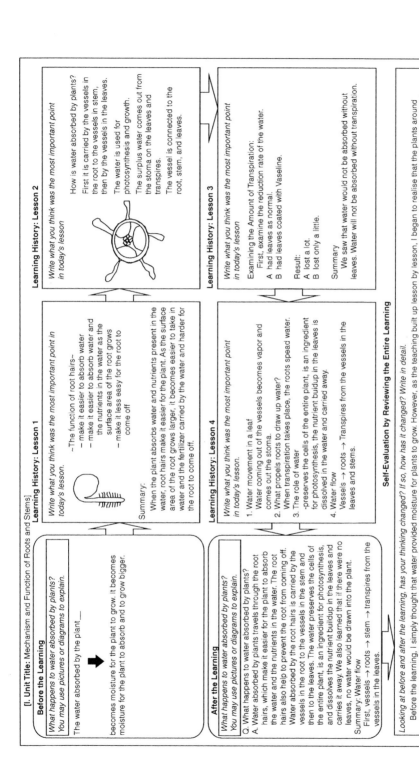

[I. Unit Title: Mechanism and Function of Roots and Stems]

**Before the Learning**

*What happens to water absorbed by plants? You may use pictures or diagrams to explain.*

The water absorbed by the plant___

becomes moisture for the plant to grow. It becomes moisture for the plant to absorb and to grow bigger.

**Learning History: Lesson 1**

*Write what you think was the most important point in today's lesson.*

~The function of root hairs~
 – make it easier to absorb water
 – make it easier to absorb water and the nutrients in the water as the surface area of the root grows
 – make it less easy for the root to come off

Summary:
When the plant absorbs water and nutrients present in the water, root hairs make it easier for the plant. As the surface area of the root grows larger, it becomes easier to take in water and the fertilizer carried by the water and harder for the root to come off.

**Learning History: Lesson 2**

*Write what you think was the most important point in today's lesson*

How is water absorbed by plants?
First it is carried by the vessels in the root to the vessels in stem, then by the vessels in the leaves.

The water is used for photosynthesis and growth.

The surplus water comes out from the stoma on the leaves and transpires.

The vessel is connected to the root, stem, and leaves.

**After the Learning**

*What happens to water absorbed by plants? You may use pictures or diagrams to explain.*

Q. What happens to water absorbed by plants?
A. Water absorbed by plants travels through the root hairs, which make it easier for the plant to absorb the water and the nutrients in the water. The root hairs also help to prevent the root from coming off. Water absorbed by the root hairs is carried by the vessels in the root to the vessels in the stem and then to the leaves. The water preserves the cells of the entire plant, is an ingredient for photosynthesis, and dissolves the nutrient buildup in the leaves and carries it away. We also learned that if there were no leaves, no water would be drawn into the plant.

Summary: Water flow
First, vessels → roots → stem → transpires from the vessels in the leaves.

**Learning History: Lesson 4**

*Write what you think was the most important point in today's lesson.*

1. Water movement in a leaf
Water coming out of the vessels becomes vapor and comes out the stoma.
2. What propels roots to draw up water?
When transpiration takes place, the roots spead water.
3. The role of water
 – preserves the cells of the entire plant, is an ingredient for photosynthesis, the nutrient buidup in the leaves is dissolved in the water and carried away.
4. Water flow
Vessels → roots → Transpires from the vessels in the leaves and stems.

**Learning History: Lesson 3**

*Write what you think was the most important point in today's lesson*

Examining the Amount of Transpiration:
First, examine the reduction rate of the water.
A  had leaves as normal.
B  had leaves coated with Vaseline.

Result:
A  lost a lot.
B  lost only a little.

Summary
We saw that water would not be absorbed without leaves. Water will not be absorbed without transpiration.

**Self-Evaluation by Reviewing the Entire Learning**

*Looking at before and after the learning, has your thinking changed? If so, how has it changed? Write in detail.*

Before the learning, I simply thought that water provided moisture for plants to grow. However, as the teaching built up lesson by lesson, I began to realise that the plants around me were quite fascinating. At first, I was not really interested in this topic, but the lessons became very enjoyable. I am surprised at the change that took place in me. One thing that I learned was to hope that I can become someone who does not start out with thinking something as boring but makes an effort to enjoy the learning process.

Figure 8.2  Example OPP sheet entries for "Mechanism and Function of Roots and Stems"

Source: Hori, 2011, p. 60

to utilise the results in their teaching. Students can visibly track their growth following this specific information. It is thought to foster the ability to learn and think independently in students.

Usually for OPPA, one OPP sheet is created to grade each unit's lesson plan. Next, students are made to fill in their learning record after each class. Teachers review these sheets by making appropriate comments and attempt to improve their learning. Through this repetition, students evaluate their learning progress as a whole after each unit is completed. It is a method that makes students evaluate themselves.

I will explain the essential structure on which this is based.

An OPP sheet is organised into four parts: "I. Unit Title," "II. Essential Questions Before and After the Learning," "III. Learning History," and "IV. Self-Evaluation after the Learning."

The teacher may write down "I. Unit Title," although some teachers have the students write it down after the unit is complete. This is to improve their ability to reflect on the whole unit and summarise it accurately.

## 4–2 The initiative of educational assessment in participation of students

It can also be said that the combination of objective-referenced assessment and intra-individual assessment plays the position of encouraging participation among students in educational assessment. For a long time, educational assessment has been thought of as a possession of the teachers or as a last resort; therefore, this opinion has a particularly radical personality. However, it would be no exaggeration to observe that a subjective class creation, premised by ignoring or rejecting student participation in educational assessment, has the potential to remain superficial or even in the realms of fantasy.

Granted, just because this is emphasised, it does not mean that the relationship between the teacher and student will turn sour. For example, the scene of a conference in a portfolio assessment, which is just a typical assessment method indicating the combination of objective-referenced assessment and intra-individual assessment, is a scene where the teacher and student share the experience of examining the quality (standard) of the work. Here, both the teacher and student are keenly aware that educational assessment is a shared experience. Furthermore, the participation in educational assessment extends to the guardians and people of the region. Regarding this point, it can easily be understood when remembering the role of the guardian or the people of the region in the recent integrated study. Innevitably, when various people begin to participate in influencing educational assessment in this way, the specialty of the teacher and how the different participating views in the process can coexist will come into question.

Now, with relative assessment gone from the cumulative guidance record revised in 2001, educational reforms provided by PISA are on a global scale, and it has become a symbol of the globalisation of education. From the standpoint of educational assessment research, and because PISA is the sure standard for educational research and educational assessment, the focus is now on the authentic assessment theory as the basis for educational assessment theory. Notably, after the PISA Shock in 2004, once the ability to think/judge/express utilizing knowledge and skill was emphasised, performance assessment in the subjects is beginning to spread. By continuing to be influenced by the authentic assessment of the United States, a rich practice reflecting the accumulation of lesson research of Japan is being created.

Although it was a bit of a hassle, I have generalised the walks of post-war educational assessment theory centred on epoch-making. In the 21st century, and in the state of relative assessment finally being swept away from the cumulative guidance records, the theories and methods of educational assessment are able to stand on a new stage. That is, in the various situations of education in practice of educational assessment called the combination of objective-referenced assessment and intra-individual assessment, the goal is to specify the education system to various levels. In this meaning, educational assessment is becoming one of the most fascinating research fields of education study.

## References

Hori, T. (2003). *Educational Assessment of Science that Cultivates the Meaning of Learning* [Manabi no Imi wo sodateru rika no Kyoiku hyoka]. Tokyo: Toyokan Publishing.

Hori, T. (2011). The Concept and Effectiveness of Teaching Practices Using OPPA. In Japanese Educational Research Association (JERA) (Ed.). *Educational Studies in Japan: International Yearbook*. No. 6. Tokyo: JERA, pp. 47–67.

Ishii, T. (2011). *Development of Academic Formation Theory in Modern America* [Gendai America ni okeru Gakuryoku keisei-ron no tenkai]. Tokyo: Toshindo Publishing.

Itakura, K. (1971). Setting of Curriculum and Academic Research [Kyoiku-katei no Settei to Gakuryoku-Chosa]. In Itakura, K. (Ed.). *Science and Hypothesis* [Kagaku to Kasetsu]. Tokyo: Hino Shobou, pp. 346–7.

Nakauchi, T. (1971). *Theory of Academic Ability and Assessment* [Gakuryoku to hyoka no riron]. Tokyo: Kokudosha.

Nishioka, K. (2003). *Utilizing Portfolio Assessment in Subjects and Integrated Studies* [Kyoka to Sogo ni ikasu Portfolio hyoka-hou]. Tokyo: Toshobunka.

Smith, E.R., Tyler, R.W., and the Evaluation Staff (1942). *Appraising and Recording Student*. New York: Harper & Brothers.

Tanaka, K. (2008). *Educational Assessment* [Kyoiku hyoka]. Tokyo: Iwanami Shoten.

# Chapter 9

# Portfolio assessment in the period for integrated study

*Kanae Nishioka*

## Introduction

The introduction of the Period for Integrated Study (PFIS) in the revised National Courses of Study (NCS) in 1998 played a major role in advancing the reform of the assessment of academic achievement in Japan. The PFIS aims to help students develop qualities and abilities to identify tasks, learn and think on their own, proactively make decisions and better solve problems. In other words, the PFIS values students' proactive engagement in inquiry activities.

Since it is clear that conventional written tests cannot be used for assessment in the PFIS, portfolio assessment has begun to attract attention. Many books were published regarding portfolio assessment from the late 1990s to the early 2000s in Japan. With Koji Tanaka, who is the co-author of this book, I published a book proposing methods of utilising portfolio assessment taking into consideration the theoretical and practical knowledge on portfolio assessment accumulated in the United States (Tanaka and Nishioka, 1999). I also conducted joint research with Ms. Hiroko Miyamoto, who teaches at the Fuzoku elementary school attached to Naruto University of Education, regarding how to utilise portfolio assessment in the PFIS, and published a book to introduce such practices (Miyamoto, Nishioka, and Sera, 2004).

In this chapter, I will first reiterate the definition and key points of portfolio assessment as I understand it and then outline basic points for promoting portfolio assessment in the PFIS. In addition, I will introduce how portfolio assessment is actually utilised in Japan by presenting the example of Ms. Miyamoto's implementation of portfolio assessment in the PFIS.

## I What is portfolio assessment?

### I–I Definition

The term 'portfolio' here refers to the systematic accumulation of records of a student's work and self-assessment as well as the teacher's guidance and assessment. Portfolio assessment is an approach in which teachers encourage students to self-assess how their learning should be through the creation of a portfolio while the teachers themselves assess each student's learning activities as well as their own teaching activities (Nishioka, 2003).

Portfolios can be used by students of various ages. Figure 9.1 (1) is a portfolio created by an elementary school student. The portfolio has a sleeve for each assessment item in the cumulative guidance record by school subject. The

*Figure 9.1* Portfolios in educational settings

(1) Elementary school student's portfolio (cf. Miyamoto, 2004)

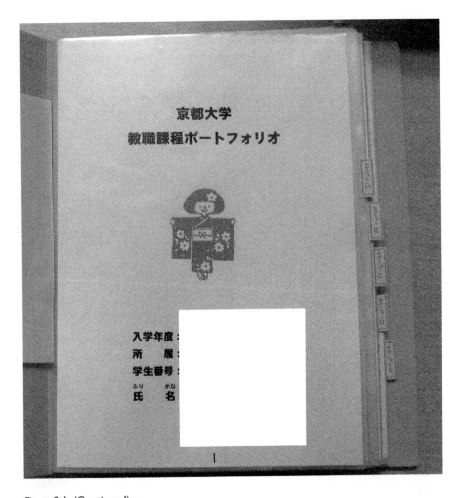

京都大学
教職課程ポートフォリオ

入学年度 :
所　　属 :
学生番号 :
ふり　　がな
氏　　名

*Figure 9.1* (Continued)
(2) Teacher training course portfolio (cf. Nishioka, Ishii, Kawaji, and Kitahara, 2013)

materials generated when students achieved a sense of mastery of a given evaluation item were added to replace the old materials from the prior trimester
(cf. Miyamoto, 2004).

Figure 9.1 (2), on the other hand, is a teacher training course portfolio created by a university student working toward a teacher's licence. In this type of
portfolio, students are required to accumulate evidence demonstrating that they
have acquired the competency required of a teacher while completing the teacher
training course at the university. It is organised such that the cover page, table
of contents, the report written at the time of completion of the teacher training
course, assessment criteria (rubrics, checklists, etc.) and the Academic Year-based

Goal Setting and Review sheet are compiled at the beginning, and documentation of achievement is compiled according to five pillars such as the 'ability to understand students and build human relationships' and 'competency in teaching practice for course subjects' (cf. Nishioka, Ishii, Kawaji, and Kitahara, 2013).

### 1–2 Portfolio ownership

When using portfolios in educational settings, it is necessary to first consider the question 'Why create a portfolio?'– i.e., the purpose, in addition to ownership. Ownership refers to the right to decide which materials are included in the portfolio and what criteria and standards are used for their assessment (Nishioka, 2003).

Directing our attention to ownership first, we see that portfolios can be divided roughly into the following three types.

(a) Best work portfolio: The collected materials as well as the criteria and standards to evaluate them are determined by the student.
(b) Criteria creation portfolio: The collected materials as well as the criteria and standards to evaluate them are determined through negotiations between the teacher and student.
(c) Criteria compliant portfolio: The collected materials as well as the criteria and standards to evaluate them are predetermined by educators.

'Portfolio' originally refers to folders, files, scrapbooks, etc. that are used by painters, architects, newspaper reporters and other professionals when they are selling their services to a client. Painters may include materials to showcase their masterpieces, exhibition brochures and reviews published in the newspaper, for example. A painter's competency, style and even level of social recognition can be clearly seen in his or her portfolio.

It is (a) the best work portfolio that is modelled after this type of professional portfolio. In a best work portfolio, students basically keep what they want to retain. The advantages of this include being able to capture the state of learning from the perspective of students themselves and help students form their identities. Needless to say, students can use their portfolio to promote their qualifications when advancing to higher education or securing employment.

As mentioned, it was the introduction of the PFIS that led to the portfolio becoming commonplace in elementary and middle schools in Japan. In the PFIS, objectives are defined through discussions between the student and teacher during the process of engaging in inquiry. In this learning process, it is effective to use (b) the criteria creation portfolio.

When conducting an assessment based on objectives in subject-based education, it is effective to use (c) the criteria compliant portfolio. Specifying the work to be delivered or assessment criteria for a given objective allows stakeholders such as the teacher, student and parents to share a clear understanding of how academic achievement is evaluated.

Notably, general-purpose skills developed across school subjects have been attracting attention in recent years in Japan as well. It is conceivable that using portfolios will make cross-curriculum evaluation possible. For example, educators could use methods such as accumulating records of the works created when students demonstrate logical thinking or communication skills across the curriculum.

As described, portfolios can be used for a variety of purposes. It is important to choose a type that serves the purpose when designing a portfolio. That said, classifying portfolios into the three types shown above is not always straightforward. For example, the two cases of portfolios shown in Figure 9.1 were also created by the teacher determining the framework to some extent while incorporating parts that were left to the student's discretion.

### 1–3 Points in providing guidance

Regardless of what type of portfolio is used, the following three points of guidance should be followed.

The first is to have a shared vision between the student and teacher. The portfolio should be created after first arriving at a shared understanding of why the portfolio is being created, what is the point of creating it, what work should be retained, when and how much time should be spent creating the portfolio, how the portfolio will be utilised and so on.

Secondly, it is necessary to set aside time to edit the accumulated works. This could include tasks such as organising materials to create a table of contents and writing an introduction and conclusion. One can also take the approach of choosing only the necessary works from the working portfolio, to which materials are added on daily basis, and transferring them to the permanent portfolio. Note that creating opportunities for students to show the portfolio can increase their motivation to organise it as they prepare for the presentation.

Third, it is important to hold a portfolio conference on regular basis. 'Portfolio conference' refers to a forum for stakeholders to use the portfolio and have a discussion about its contents. Dialogues may take place at a portfolio conference in the following manner, for example.

(1) Prompt self-assessment from the student by asking open-ended questions.
(2) Listen to the student talk (patiently wait until he/she begins).
(3) Check for the achievements demonstrated in the items collected and praise them.
(4) Allow the student to intuitively grasp the objectives and criteria by comparing specific examples.

(5)  Discuss and agree on the next objectives.
(6)  Take notes about confirmed achievements, tasks and objectives.

A conference offers not only a place for students to present their learning accomplishments but also an opportunity to look ahead at future milestones, issues and objectives.

To restate these three points from the perspective of students who drive the creation of the portfolio, it can be said that a portfolio should be made by paying attention to three points, 'whether the vision is clear', 'when and how to organise the documents' and 'how to secure the opportunity for a conference'.

## 2  Utilisation of portfolios in the PFIS

### 2–1  Study unit structure in the PFIS

Next, we will summarise the main points on how portfolio assessment is actually used in the PFIS.

Whereas in school subjects, problems and tasks are systematically organised by teachers in order for students to effectively and efficiently achieve the objectives, in the PFIS, students are required to identify issues and inquire into matters on their own. However, it is rare that students can define a good question from the beginning. The PFIS aims to help them develop the abilities to formulate a question and define research tasks on their own.

Therefore, the PFIS often adopts the type of unit structure shown in Figure 9.2. First, a common, broad theme is established for the students' grade or class while taking into account factors such as teachers' desires, students' development and regional conditions. For example, the broad theme might be 'Let's think about food in Japan' or 'Let's create a plan for community development'. The broad theme must be attractive to students as well as expandable so that diverse students can choose their own approach. Furthermore, since the PFIS also considers it important for students to have direct experiences such as conducting a field investigation, holding an interview, creating a product, or conducting an experiment, it is desirable to have a broad theme that can meet the conditions for them to have such experiences. At the same time, it is necessary to establish a broad theme that can lead to some sort of controversy in the course of the inquiry and allow students to focus on modern issues such as the environment and social welfare.

Next, the introduction of the unit is designed to engage students in the broad theme. For example, the teacher may offer students opportunities to promote their critical awareness of food issues or let them meet people from the community who are experiencing some kind of difficulty. In this way, each student can find some kind of 'question' related to the broad theme. In order to utilise portfolios, it is also important to explain the benefits of portfolios and how to create one at the introduction stage.

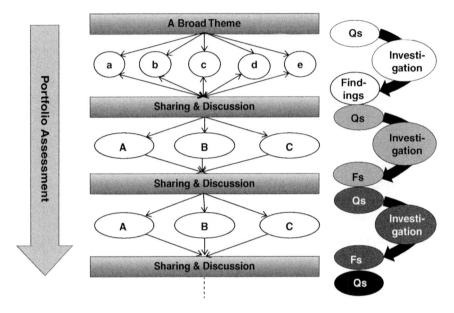

*Figure 9.2* Unit structure in the PFIS

Source: Nishioka, 2003, p. 103

Note: Q: question; F: finding

At the stage of unit implementation, the problem-solving cycle of 'identifying a question, conducting an investigation and making a new discovery while the next question surfaces' is repeated several times. For this, it is a good idea to plan the order of activities so that students are alternately engaged in individual or group activities and discussion time or sharing. Individual students' discoveries and questions are examined during sharing time when discussions are held in groups or as a whole class. Focusing on similarities and differences between these discoveries and questions can help define a new task. When the task is redefined many times, the inquiry is gradually expanded. It is also important to plan at the implementation stage when and in what format to hold a portfolio conference.

In the inquiry process, multiple opportunities to summarise and present student achievements should be provided: e.g., an intermediate conference to look back on the learning outcomes so far and to think about how to move forward or a presentation to show the achievements to students in other grades, parents and people in the community.

### 2–2 Places to utilise portfolios and the viewpoints on assessment

There are three major times to utilise this type of portfolio as part of the guidance offered in the PFIS. The first is when the broad theme is set. The PFIS requires teachers to design a unit in accordance with students' developmental stages and readiness. If individual students are already developing sufficient critical awareness of the issue, the teacher can let them conduct an inquiry based on that awareness. However, if the students have not yet developed sufficient critical awareness of the issue, the teacher might assign a common broad theme to be investigated by all students in the grade level or class. To what extent the students are aware of the issue can be assessed based on the portfolios they created in the previous grade.

The second time is at the portfolio conference that takes place during the inquiry process. Students can bring their portfolios with materials they have accumulated since the beginning of the unit. The teacher would then pose questions such as 'What are you interested in? Why?' 'How are you conducting the research?' 'What have you discovered so far?' and 'What difficulties are you experiencing?' The students would report on what they were able to accomplish and what difficulties they faced based on the materials accumulated in the portfolio. The students and teacher would reflect on these conditions and plan together how to proceed with the next inquiry.

In the PFIS, conferences can be held in rotation during the individual/group activities. Holding one individual or group conference per semester or trimester would allow the teacher to understand each student's progress well. In addition, teachers can structurally organise students' remarks on the blackboard to help them notice similarities and differences and identify new questions, thereby encouraging them to define tasks for the next inquiry. In any case, it is necessary to look through the students' portfolios in advance and plan what questions to ask, how to elicit remarks from the students and organise them on the blackboard and so on.

The third time is when the students themselves edit their portfolios. For example, it is effective to have students review the materials collected in their own portfolios and think about their achievements and tasks prior to the conference. The teacher can also ask students to think about key points to emphasise in the presentation while selecting the most important materials from the portfolio when preparing for the presentation.

As a note, the progress of the inquiry and growth of student's ability in the PFIS can be understood by consistently using the same point of view and conducting repeated assessments. Specifically, the following five points can be considered.

- What issues has the student noticed? What is the quality of the question the student is investigating?
- Is the student thinking logically? Did he/she formulate steps in the inquiry that are consistent with the theme? Has he/she noticed the relationship, commonalities and differences between matters? Has he/she considered the issue by synthesising various information?
- Is he/she having a direct experience such as creating something, interviewing, experimenting, or conducting a field survey? Is he/she avoiding blindly accepting and copying ideas from books or the Internet?

- Is he/she demonstrating the ability to collaborate? Is he/she cooperating in the group? Is he/she capable of using other students' opinions to create a new idea?
- Has he/she learnt how to accurately assess him/herself?

Furthermore, it is important to pay attention to whether students are successfully expanding their inquiries utilising, as needed, the knowledge, skills and understanding that they should have already learnt in school subjects, which is the aim of the PFIS. The importance of knowledge, skills and understanding learnt in school subjects will also become clear during the course of the inquiry in the PFIS. Ideally, learning in the PFIS enhances what students learn in school subjects and vice versa.

## 3 A practical example: The fourth-grade unit 'the broader world we see from Shiroyama'

### 3–1 Establishing a broad theme and introducing the unit

This section introduces how portfolio assessment was implemented by a teacher, Ms. Hiroko Miyamoto. First, Ms. Miyamoto chose Shiroyama, a natural woodland near the school, as a field for her fourth-grade students and set 'The Broader World We See from Shiroyama' as the broad theme. To start the school year, she looked through the students' portfolios from previous years to understand the extent of their critical awareness of the issue. Since each of the sixth graders she taught the previous year had developed a considerable level of critical awareness of the issue, she instructed each of these students to think of their own task for the inquiry. However, for the fourth-grade students, she decided to use Shiroyama, which is located near the school and is very familiar to the students, as a common theme for the class.

The fourth-grade students were asked to define their own tasks to investigate 'The Broader World We See from Shiroyama'. However, at first, they were unable to precisely define a task from scratch. For example, one student initially defined his task as 'interview people who come to Shiroyama'. Ms. Miyamoto said, 'Let's go to Shiroyama and see if the tasks everyone thought of are actually doable' and took the students out. After visiting Shiroyama, the students reconsidered their tasks, saying, for example, 'I wrote that I wanted to interview people, but what do I want to interview them about?' Ultimately, the student mentioned above redefined the task as 'interview people who come to Shiroyama in order to investigate what about Shiroyama appeals to them'. In this way, the students selected their subjects, such as insects, animals, humans and history, and proceeded to investigate these topics by teaming up with other students who had chosen similar subjects.

### 3–2 Dialogues at the conference

In this way, the students began investigating the subject that they chose as a group; however, the inquiry did not progress smoothly. Therefore, Ms. Miyamoto

Ms. Miyamoto: [While looking at her notebook] You wanted to check what type of insects were living in Shiroyama, how they developed, and the manner in which they lived, correct? The great thing about Yuko was that Yuko did not forget to prepare an insect cage and net.

Tatsuya: I brought an insect cage.

Ms. Miyamoto: What was the most difficult thing for you to do in order to actually complete this work? [Tatsuya and Yuko took some time to review their portfolios.] What was the hardest part?

Yuko: There were only butterflies. I was looking for other insects. But I could not find them; some of those I found were already dead.

Tatsuya: [Pulling out a map of Shiroyama from the portfolio and pointing at it.] Teacher, we went all over these places, but I could find nothing there. There are normally butter flies and drone beetles around. But when I went there, I couldn't even find any butterflies. So, I gave up trying to find them around there and went down....[Omission]

Ms. Miyamoto: So, the flight patterns of the butterflies were not very clear [taking notes in her notebook], and thus you could not check them, right?

Tatsuya: Yes. [Yuko nods.]

Ms. Miyamoto: You need to figure out some tricks for this kind of checking. You can think about this in many ways. [Hears Akemi muttering 'I got it'.] Did you get it? What kind of tricks?

Akemi: Well, I don't know if I have got it right, but when butterflies emerge, you should measure the temperature. And when you next see them, you should measure the temperature again...

Tatsuya: [Breathlessly] That's how we find them!

Ms. Miyamoto: What Akemi said right now is one method. [Toru raises his hand.] Do you have an opinion? [Toru nods.] Yes.

Toru: [Becoming excited] I am thinking about different ways to eat or slurp foods, such as watermelons. I think it would be great to lure butterflies using bait and then define the shapes of their mouths with a magnifying glass.

Tatsuya: I see!

Ms. Miyamoto: You have a point there. In fact, Toru, Akemi, and Tatsuya each gave different goals, in the sense that they have different approaches toward narrowing down this work. Observing the way of imbibing food was Toru's idea, and this approach focused on how the insect eats, as well as the characteristics and movements of a single insect. Meanwhile, Akemi mentioned relationships with temperature and wind that can indicate places where insects may be found. [After the aforementioned procedures, the teacher advised the students that they needed to choose a method of studying that is based on their goal. Additionally, the teacher advised students that they could consult books about insects in the library.]

*Figure 9.3* A group conference dialogue (the student names are pseudonyms)

Source: Nishioka, 2003, p. 125

looked at the materials collected in the portfolios to understand each student's inquiry process and held a conference. Figure 9.3 shows an example of the dialogue from the group conference. The dialogue took place when Tatsuya and Yuko, who were investigating insects, consulted Ms. Miyamoto; Akemi and Toru, who were in the next group waiting for their turn, participated in the dialogue as well.

When the conference took place, Tatsuya was stuck in terms of how to investigate insects, although he initially had a clear desire to research them. In the dialogue, three ideas were suggested regarding how he could investigate insects, and Tatsuya responded positively each time. Tatsuya would have continued with the same type of inquiry activities if it had not been for the guidance of Ms. Miyamoto. Which one of the three ideas should be used was a decision for Tatsuya himself to make according to his objective. However, he needed the teacher's guidance to help him choose the inquiry method based on the objective. Tatsuya also became interested in a new method of library research through the advice of the teacher.

As this dialogue shows, the teacher's guidance in the PFIS emphasises how to identify the direction of the inquiry based on what the student has already learnt so that the previous learning is utilised. Furthermore, Ms. Miyamoto's guidance is characterised by the fact that she clarifies the next objective of choosing a research method according to the purpose by relating all remarks from the participating students at the conference without negating them.

Moreover, the questions Ms. Miyamoto posed at the group conference varied by the stage of the unit in the PFIS. She emphasised points such as 'how to define what you noticed or wondered about as a topic' and 'whether it seems feasible to collect materials corresponding to the defined topic' during her guidance at the beginning of the unit. If the students were in the middle of the unit, she questioned points such as 'whether materials are steadily collected', 'whether the students understand each item in their own words', and 'what is the redefined task as a result of the focus that emerged from the collected information'. At the summary stage of the unit, the students were instructed to think about what they wanted to communicate the most about their discoveries and how they could communicate it well.

### 3–3 Classroom discussions and organisation using the blackboard

At Japanese schools with large class sizes, there is a limit to the amount of guidance that can be given at each conference. For this reason, Ms. Miyamoto decided to hold a conference in the form of instruction given to the whole class. Specifically, an interim presentation was held as part of the preparation for the final presentation to parents.

Prior to the interim presentation, Ms. Miyamoto looked at the students' portfolios and considered what kind of guidance she could give to further enhance the contents in preparation for the final presentation. In the lesson to prepare for the interim presentation, she instructed the students to review the materials accumulated in the portfolio and, in their groups, summarise the results of the inquiry on a simple poster. She also prepared cards that indicated the topic each group worked on.

At the beginning of the interim presentation, Ms. Miyamoto instructed the class to think about similarities and differences between the contents of the group presentations when listening to each other because the purpose of the lesson was to think about the organisation of the final presentation. Once some groups had shown their posters and given their presentations to the rest of the class, the teacher said 'Let's combine similar ideas' and posed questions such as 'Which groups would become more powerful when linked together?' and 'What combinations might make opinions even better?' She instructed the students to put the cards that listed the group topics on the blackboard and connect them with lines to indicate their relevance to each other.

Figure 9.4 shows a scene from this lesson. The students thought about similarities and differences and made remarks while listening to each other's presentations. As can be seen, although their remarks were initially about apparent classifications, the students gradually came to grasp the associations between the group presentations and ultimately thought about the contents they wanted to convey in the final presentation. In this way, the organisation shown in Figure 9.5 was created at the end.

Subsequently, group conferences were held in order to further polish the presentation contents for each group according to the organisation identified in the interim presentation. The final presentation was given on 'parents' day', and each student gave a creative presentation. At the end, the unit was concluded by students' organising the portfolio and reflecting on the meaning of their own learning.

---

Toru: How about dividing into nature and humans? The groups doing insects, birds, and plants are the nature group, and the ones researching garbage and workers are the human group.

Keiko: If so, the group doing air falls under both. Wind is natural, but things like smell and exhaust gas are deeply related to humans.

Saori: I've researched waste in Shiroyama, but waste, leaves, and branches in Shiroyama become mulch and return to nature. So you can't separate them. [...]

Satoru: Maybe we can create a group called 'What we want to do with Shiroyama in the future'.

Saki: How about a group called 'How humans have been involved with the mountain'?

Saori: That includes two types: 'What humans have done to nature' and 'What nature has given to humans'.

Kohei: Shiroyama has a mix of natural and artificial things. It's neither nature nor human.

Ms. Miyamoto: There are groups that captured the fact that nature is interrelated. There are groups that captured the fact that humans and nature are involved with each other. The group doing trees is one of them, isn't it? Trees that live in nature, trees that live in the artificial [environment]. And since trees were already being deliberately planted and used when the Tokushima Castle was constructed, those trees can also be regarded as trees living in an artificial environment created by humans.

Miki: Sometimes the way of life of animals and plants is changed by humans. Sometimes it's changed by the natural environment. I wonder which is affecting the growth of trees.

Akemi: But I don't think our group [the group that interviewed people who came to Tokushima Park] falls under any of them. [...]

---

*Figure 9.4* A group conference dialogue (the student names are pseudonyms)

Source: Miyamoto, 2004, p. 59

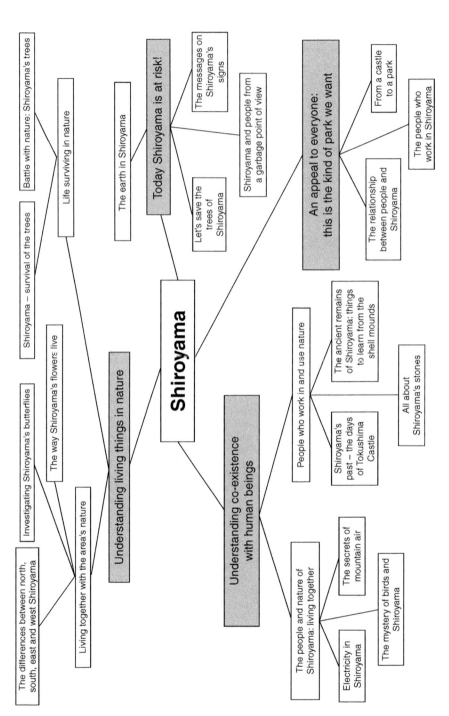

*Figure 9.5* Example of blackboard map from the unit "The Broader World We See from Shiroyama"

Source: Miyamoto, 2004, p. 60

The students engaged in an inquiry in the unit 'The Broader World We See from Shiroyama', then investigated the Yoshino River in the unit 'Tales Told by the Yoshino River: The Environment and Me' in the second and third trimesters, respectively. The tasks they defined this time were much more precise compared to those at the beginning of the school year. For example, Tatsuya, who was investigating insects, learned that butterflies in Shiroyama flew up and down the mountain during the day. When starting the inquiry about the Yoshino River, he was already capable of defining a task, as indicated in his statement, 'I'm interested in the migration of animals. Since I've heard that sweetfish ascend and descend the Yoshino River over a lifetime, I want to investigate sweetfish in the Yoshino River'. We can say that the example of Tatsuya plainly shows that the PFIS can improve a student's ability to define tasks.

## Conclusion

Portfolios are used mainly in school subject education and career education in the United Kingdom and United States. In Japan, the introduction of the PFIS prompted the spread of portfolio assessment.

Ms. Miyamoto's teaching practice shows that using portfolios in the PFIS enables the teacher to teach students to suit their learning process. For example, students used portfolios at the group conference to report their progress and explain where they were stuck. The teacher assisted by advising them to narrow down the issue and suggesting inquiry methods. She also enhanced the students' learning during the class discussions by instructing them to utilise the materials they had accumulated in the portfolio in preparation for the presentation and relate them with each other's presentation contents. In this process, it was particularly effective to show a map of the ideas on the blackboard in order to organise the students' thoughts.

The PFIS aims to help students develop the abilities to define questions on their own and pursue an inquiry. A portfolio conference held in the form of a group conference or classroom discussion is particularly beneficial for this purpose.

## References

Miyamoto, H. (2004). "Integrated study for fourth graders: 'The broader world we see from Shiroyama' and 'Tales told by Yoshino River' [Yo-nensei no Sogo Gakushu: 'Shiroyama kara hirogaru sekai' to 'Yoshinogawa wa kataru']". In Miyamoto, H., Nishioka, K. & Sera, H. (Eds.), *Portfolio assessment for developing comprehensive learning ability in integrated study and subjects: Implementation* [Sogo to kyoka no tashikana gakuryoku wo hagukumu portfolio hyoka-hou: jissen-hen]. Tokyo: Nihon Hyoujun, pp. 125–44.

Miyamoto, H., Nishioka, K., & Sera, H. (2004). *Portfolio assessment for developing solid academic ability in integrated and subjects study: Implementation* [Sogo to kyoka no tashikana gakuryoku wo hagukumu portfolio hyoka-hou]. Tokyo: Nihon Hyoujun.

Nishioka, K. (2003). *Portfolio assessment utilised in subjects and integrated study* [Kyoka to sogo ni ikasu portfolio hyoka-hou]. Tokyo: Toshobunka.

Nishioka, K., Ishii, T., Kawaji, A., & Kitahara, T. (2013). *Workbook of a practical seminar for the teaching profession: Improve your teaching competencies by using a portfolio* [Kyosyoku jissen ensyu workbook: Portfolio de Kyoshi-ryoku up]. Kyoto: Minerva Shobo.

Tanaka, K., & Nishioka, K. (1999). *Integrated study and portfolio assessment: Introduction* [Sogo gakushu to portfolio hyoka-hou: nyumon-hen]. Tokyo: Nihon Hyoujun.

# Chapter 10

# Performance assessment in subject teaching

*Kanae Nishioka*

## Introduction

The 1998 revised National Courses of Study (NCS) postulated a curriculum in which students acquire knowledge and skills within subjects and engage in inquiries during the Period for Integrated Study (PFIS). In reality, however, it was difficult for students to engage in such inquiries. Following the startling results of the 2004 Programme for International Student Assessment (PISA), commonly referred to as the 'PISA shock', the importance of students' abilities to utilise knowledge and skills in real-life contexts was acknowledged. The 2008 revised NCS announced the policy of considering scholastic abilities from the perspective of the three factors of 'basic and fundamental knowledge and skills', 'abilities to think, to make decisions, and to express oneself, and other abilities that are necessary to solve problems', and 'an attitude of proactive learning', with the second factor necessary for utilising the first factor to resolves issues (Nishioka, 2009a, Cf. Director-General, Elementary and Secondary Education Bureau, the Ministry of Education, Culture, Sports, Science and Technology, 2010).

Within the context of the above developments, I have been conducting collaborative studies with teachers to develop practices that incorporate performance tasks within subject-based education. The achievements of these collaborative studies have been evaluated highly and are being paid close attention to within discussions of the next NCS revision.

This chapter will discuss how performance tasks can be incorporated in subject-based education by presenting concrete practical examples. The teaching practices of Ms. Asami Mifuji, a teacher, during a middle school social studies class will be mainly discussed (Mifuji, 2010). This chapter will also introduce various methods used during classes, including worksheet assignments, writing on the blackboard, group work, and debate sessions.

## I Corresponding educational objectives and assessment methods

### I–I Significance and issues of 'objective-referenced assessment'

In Japan, the concept of 'objective-referenced assessment' was adopted across the board in the 2001 revised cumulative guidance record. A cumulative guidance record is defined as 'a record on the student's school register and the summary of the guidance process and results, which will later serve as a ledger used for future guidance and providing evidence for external bodies. It is a register which becomes significant when proceeding with learning assessments in a planned manner at each school'. As such, its creation is compulsory for all schools.

Objective-referenced assessment is greatly significant because it promotes the clarification of objectives, assessment criteria and standards before teaching starts, and it enables improvements to be made to instruction based on assessments made according to the objectives. Objective-reference assessment consists of three types of assessment: diagnostic, formative and summative. Diagnostic assessment reveals students' preparedness for learning before they begin education. Formative assessment is conducted to improve the guidance offered to students by verifying the outcome of education during its process. Summative assessment is carried out at the end of teaching practice to assign grades based on students' scholastic abilities as a whole. In particular, the enhancement of diagnostic and formative assessments can contribute to securing the scholastic abilities of all students.

At the same time, various questions arise in objective-referenced assessment, such as 'How do we set objectives and assessment standards?' 'What kinds of assessment methods should be used?' and 'How can we improve guidance based on assessments?' Furthermore, when giving detailed guidance appropriate for each student, teachers should use a combination of objective-referenced assessment and individual assessment. Specific strategies for clarifying this process are needed.

In Japan, the development of specific assessment standards is reviewed and done at each school. I have been introducing the curriculum design methodology advocated in *Understanding by Design* (Wiggins & McTighe, 1998; Wiggins & McTighe, 2005; hereafter, UbD) as an approach that provides an overview during this development process. UbD advocates planning the following as a trio: (1) desired results (goals), (2) acceptable evidence (assessment methods) and (3) learning experience and instruction (how learning and instruction proceed). This idea is referred to as 'backward design'. This is because, in this approach, the assessment methods that are usually planned only after the teacher has given the students guidance are instead arranged before the guidance is given. As such, education is designed retroactively from the ultimate results produced at the end of a unit/grade or at and after graduation.

### 1–2 Various methods for scholastic ability assessment

According to UbD, selecting and developing appropriate assessment methods first by reviewing the objective becomes a key in the development of subject curricula. This section will verify the methods of assessing academic achievements.

Figure 10.1 shows my classification of various methods of assessing scholastic ability that heretofore have been developed. The figure lists assessment methods ranging from the simple to the complex and categorises evaluations into those based on written material versus demonstration.

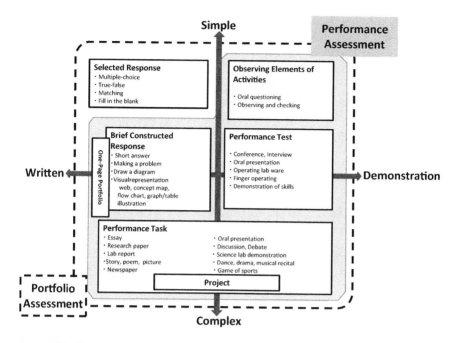

*Figure 10.1*   Assessment methods

Source: Nishioka, 2009b. Cf. McTighe & Ferrara, 1998.

Assessment methods are generally presumed to consist of **written tests** or **performance tests**. There have also been various problems and tasks developed for testing methods. Selected response format questions (objective testing method), in which the markers check whether the answers are either 'right' or 'wrong', are suitable for evaluating whether a wide range of knowledge has been acquired and within a large group of people in a limited time. However, written tests with free-description type questions or ones that incorporate performance tests are critical in the evaluation of scholastic abilities such as the abilities to think, form judgements and express oneself.

Furthermore, daily assessments that do not utilise a testing method, such as checking notebooks and worksheets during class and monitoring or observing children's statements or activities, are also significant assessment methods that capture children's learning in a natural setting.

Performance tasks are a more complex assessment method that can include written descriptions or physical demonstrations. The term 'performance task' refers to a complex task that requires comprehensive mastery of various forms of knowledge and skills. More specifically, such tasks include completion of pieces (i.e., products), such as essays, reports and exhibits and demonstrations (i.e., performances, in a narrow sense), such as speeches, presentations and experiments. In particular, activities where students are asked to exhibit their abilities in a realistic context (or a simulation context) are referred to as authentic performance tasks.

Additionally, 'performance assessment' is a collective term given to assessment methods that evaluate students' abilities to freely utilise knowledge and skills. Performance assessments were advocated from movements within the US criticising the selected response method (objective testing method) used in standardised tests. Therefore, the questions other than the selected response method are encircled in the shaded area. Furthermore, the portfolio assessment method is an approach based on performance. However, since there are also cases where portfolios encompass a selected response method written test, all the assessment methods in Figure 10.1 are grouped together with a dotted line.

### 1–3  Correspondence between the structure of knowledge and the assessment method

The structure of knowledge is perceived in UbD as depicted in Figure 10.2. Factual knowledge and discrete skills lie in the lowest level of the structure of knowledge. These knowledge and skills refer to the cognitive skills required to identify proper nouns, complete simple fill-in-the-blanks and discern simple causal relations. Knowledge and skills that are considered more significant than these include transferrable concepts and complex processes. 'Transfer' refers to using knowledge and skills learned in one scope in another scope. Transferable concepts include animals, plants and life cycles. Additionally, complex processes may include observing and recording using the five senses.

At an even higher level lies the 'enduring understanding' of 'principles and generalisations' acquired through being able to freely use transferable concepts and complex processes. The term 'understanding' here refers to a state in which

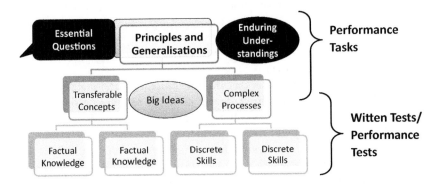

*Figure 10.2* Correspondence between the 'structure of knowledge' and assessment method

Source: Constructed based on the figure on p. 65 of McTighe & Wiggins, 2004 and the figure on p. 31 of Erickson, 2008. Wiggins & McTighe, 2005 was also referenced.

knowledge and skills can be utilised in a refined and flexible manner. Enduring understanding is then the most significant element within the concept of understanding.

In order to evaluate students' enduring understanding, it is appropriate to examine the essential questions. The essential questions are questions that are at the core of learning, as well as questions that reveal 'So what are they?' in relation to everyday life. Normally, they are questions that cannot be resolved with one simple answer. They elicit discussions and stimulate children's inquisitive nature. By positing essential questions, individuals can give associations to their knowledge and skills, which can then be integrated, and reach enduring understanding.

In relation to UbD, the essential questions are perceived in a nested structure (refer to Figure 10.3). Firstly, there are overarching essential questions that penetrate subjects, scopes and fields. Applying them to specific content in a unit can lead to capturing the essential questions for each unit. These essential questions for each unit integrate the main thought-provoking questions in each class.

Comparing this to the structure of knowledge reveals the necessity of combining various assessment methods and using them in academic achievement assessments.

## The Nested Structure of "Essential Questions"

What are happiness and peace? How is it possible to establish a peaceful and happy society?

| How do people live, and in what kinds of geographical conditions? How can we change geographical conditions? | What does the change of an era really mean? What causes change in society? What changes can create a peaceful, democratic nation and society? | What is democracy? What are the characteristics of a democratic nation? |
|---|---|---|
| | | What kind of economic problems exist? What are the causes of these problems? How can these problems be solved? |

Recurring Similar Performance Tasks

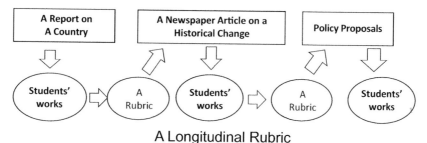

A Longitudinal Rubric

*Figure 10.3* Corresponding the nested structure of essential questions to the performance task/rubric

Source: Constructed based on the figure on p. 17 of Nishioka, 2009b and the figure on pp. 52–53 of Mifuji & Nishioka, 2010

A performance task is suitable to help determine whether or not a student has acquired enduring understanding concerning principles and generalisation. However, in order to see if individual knowledge (concepts) or skills (process) have been acquired or not, written or practical tests need to be utilised.

## 2 The development of performance tasks and rubrics

### 2–1 How to develop performance tasks

Next, we will address specifically how performance tasks are developed. When developing a performance task, it is important to first set a unit that is suitable for the performance task. In comparison to the US, Japan tends to set smaller units. In other words, the amount of time spent on a unit tends to be smaller in Japan. Since a performance task requires a certain number of hours, it is necessary to set an appropriate unit size. As there is no need to use performance tasks in all units, it is also important to select a unit suitable for employing a performance task.

Based on the UbD, the performance task is developed through the following procedure:

(1) Clarify what the essential questions are.
(2) Clarify the enduring understanding that the teachers would like the students to acquire in relation to the essential questions.
(3) Presume a context in which essential questions need to be asked, creating a scenario for a performance task.

In the process of clarifying the essential questions, it is effective to first consider what lies in the core section of the material that is to be taught to the children throughout the unit. Furthermore, it is advisable to set essential questions that are more specific for each unit in light of the instruction materials while being aware of the overarching essential questions, building upon the nested structure of essential questions.

In Ms. Mifuji's teaching practice, the questions 'What are happiness and peace? How is it possible to establish a peaceful and happy society?' were set as the overarching essential questions that were carried throughout the entire social science class during the three years of middle school. In the field of geography, the questions 'How do people live, and in what kinds of geographical conditions? How can we change geographical conditions?' were explored in accordance with each unit's subject matter. Furthermore, in history, the questions 'What does the change of an era really mean? What causes change in society? and 'What changes can create a peaceful, democratic nation and society?' were explored in the lessons on each era's turning point. The politics unit in civil studies set 'What is democracy? What are the characteristics of a democratic nation?' and the economy units placed 'What kind of economic problems exist? What are the causes of these problems? How can these problems be solved?' as the essential questions for the unit (refer to the top section of Figure 10.3).

When the essential questions for units are clarified, the kind of understanding the teacher wants students to reach in correspondence to such questions is also clarified. In the case of the economy unit, we wanted the students to understand that, 'In economy, the ideal state is for the three bodies of households, corporations and the government to serve their roles and activities smoothly, with problems arising if one of the bodies experiences a disturbance'; 'A favourable economic state is one in which the overall monetary flow is running smoothly, rather than disproportionally large profit going toward certain individuals or sectors. In order for this to happen, it is necessary to maintain a financial structure in which household budgets and corporate revenue and expenditures can easily maintain a proper balance'; and 'Furthermore, it is crucial to strengthen government policies that enhance social security policies to enable a stable economic cycle to be sustained in case it becomes difficult for households to achieve the minimum level of livelihood with their income, or for companies to conduct smooth financial activities'.

This task of clarifying enduring understanding is effective for teachers to clarify the learning objectives. However, having students memorise and reproduce these sentences as they are does not mean that the students have understood the content. Thus, students are asked to display a performance that clearly shows they understand.

UbD proposes examining the following six factors (abbreviated as GRASPS) when formulating a scenario for a performance task: The *goal* of the performance, the *role* to be simulated or fulfilled by the students, the *audience* of the performance, the presumed *situation*, *product/performance* to be produced, and the *standards/criteria for success*. Incorporating these factors, a performance task was formulated for the economy unit as shown in Figure 10.4.

### 2–2 Development of rubrics

In the development of performance tasks, the assessment standards for products and performances become an issue; performance tasks cannot be graded using 'right' or 'wrong' evaluations. Therefore, a rubric is employed. A rubric is an assessment standard chart comprised of a numerical scale that indicates the degree of success and descriptors that state the performance characteristics that correspond to each level (Nishioka, 2003).

Rubrics for a specific task can be developed using the following procedure (Cf. Wiggins, 1998).

(1) Conduct a performance task and gather performance case examples (i.e., products and performances) of students.

(2) Grade the case examples based on impressions formed from a quick observation, according to the following five levels: 5 'excellent, 4 'good', 3 'pass', 2 'needs more work', and 1 'needs a lot of improvement'. When grading is

Imagine that you are a parliament member, and elections for the House of Representatives will take place soon. TV FY will hold a series of discussions on economic policy before the election. During this program, parliament members who propose different economic policies for certain themes will discuss issues concerning each policy.

The following three themes will be discussed.
1. The reduction of economic disparity: The 'working poor' issue
    A: Further increase free competition.
    B: Enhance social security.
2. Environmental policy
    A: Prioritize global warming prevention.
    B: Prioritize overcoming international competition.
3. Food policy
    A: Further enhance trade liberalization.
    B: Improve the food self-sufficiency rate through protection of food production.

First of all, you will choose the sessions in which you will appear as parliament members, and then conduct the following tasks:
(1) Explain the issue and its underlying causes based on social structure.
(2) Propose policies for resolving the issue, while at the same time, explain the information put forth in (1).
(3) Debate the issue with other members who have made different proposals and respond to opinions and questions from general viewers who will participate in the program.
(4) At the end, using the content of the debate after it has ended, make necessary modifications, and complete a report on policy proposals

*Figure 10.4* Performance task for the economy unit: 'Propose an Economic Policy'

Source: Mifuji, 2010, pp. 31–32

carried out by several people, take measures so that the graders cannot see each other's marks, such as attaching the grades to the back of the product. When all the graders have finished grading, re-attach the label sheet to the front of the product.

(3) Ascertain what characteristics can be gleaned from the group of work that corresponds to each level to develop descriptors. In the event the descriptors are developed between several people, analysis can be started using a piece of work for which the opinions of all the graders match. If a fair amount of descriptors have been formulated, examine a work for which the opinions have split and re-formulate the descriptors so that such works can be also be appropriately evaluated.

(4) Separate the standpoints of assessment as needed and create a standpoint-based rubric.

After a rubric has been developed in this manner, case examples of a typical performance corresponding to each level (such work will be referred to here as 'anchor work') can then be prepared. Attaching anchor works to a rubric clearly indicates the characteristics of performance sought for each level.

Constructing rubrics collaboratively in this manner enables the perspective and levels of assessments to be shared. In other words, developing a rubric is an effective moderation method that heightens the comparability of assessments. Furthermore, it enables teachers to ascertain specifically which abilities they need to foster in their students and where students struggle. Through such clarification, teachers can also examine policies that can improve their guidance practices. Thus, rubric development is an effective method for improving teachers' assessment abilities.

When a performance task is employed, one can assign similar tasks repeatedly, in correspondence to the overarching essential questions (Figure 10.3). In this case, students' progress can be assessed as they make gradual improvements through multiple opportunities that surpass a unit. Such rubrics that can assess long-term growth levels are referred to as 'long-term rubrics'. By increasing the ambiguity level of the descriptors of a specific task's rubric, a long-term rubric can be developed (Nishioka, 2009b).

During Ms. Mifuji's teaching practice, performance tasks were provided in multiple units. As specific task rubrics were developed a number of times, a long-term rubric that assessed abilities to think, form judgements and express oneself through the three years of middle school was developed (Table 10.1). Having long-term rubrics in mind, Ms. Mifuji maintained awareness of the learning

*Table 10.1* Long-term rubric that assesses students' abilities to think, make decisions and express themselves

(Level 2 and Level 4 are omitted here)

| Level | Descriptors |
| --- | --- |
| 5 | In examining social phenomena, the student has more than three viewpoints, such as politics, economy, culture, population and geography. He/she is able to combine the aforementioned viewpoints in a comprehensive manner, to undertake analyses from various perspectives, to state appropriate, detailed and specific grounds for opinions, and to construct remarkably convincing assertions. Statements are made after suitable materials have been selected and compiled in a multifaceted manner. |
| 3 | In examining social phenomena, the student has more than two viewpoints, such as politics, economy, culture, population and geography. He/she is able to associate the aforementioned viewpoints, to undertake analyses from various perspectives, to mention specific grounds and to make clear assertions. Statements can be made using diverse materials. The student combines the aforementioned viewpoints and to make clear assertions by stating specific grounds for opinions. Statements are made by consulting various materials. |
| 1 | In examining social phenomena, the students states facts based on the various viewpoints, such as politics, economy, culture, population and geography. However, facts are simply listed in a fragmented manner. Difficulty in connecting assertions with grounds can be identified. Difficulties have been caused while reading and creating basic data. |

Source: Constructed based on the figure on pp. 58–59 of Mifuji & Nishioka, 2010

objective, even in new units, of having students make persuasive statements by utilising their abilities to analyse social phenomena and resources multilaterally. This awareness was then used to improve her teaching practice.

## 3 Teaching guidance measures

### 3–1  Provide an overview and make associations between daily classes and performance tasks

This section will explain key points for providing guidance to students in lessons that incorporate performance tasks and introduce the measures that Ms. Mifuji implemented when she taught the economy unit.

When incorporating performance tasks, teachers should take measures to promote students' acquisition of scholastic abilities that enable them to engage in such tasks. Figure 10.5 is a model diagram depicting how to organise the teaching of units when incorporating a performance task. In the Pattern 1 parts assembly

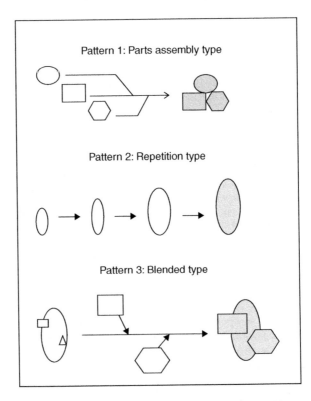

*Figure 10.5* The mapping of performance tasks: Structures within and between units
Source: Nishioka, 2008, p. 12

type, teachers have students gradually acquire the components (knowledge and skills) required for the performance task at the end of the unit. Ultimately, the students are asked to assemble the various parts. In the Pattern 2 repetition type, the quality of the task is gradually improved by having the students repeat similar tasks. In the Pattern 3 blended type, the students are first asked to complete a task once. Thereafter, guidance is given so that they can refine the necessary factors. Ultimately, the students are asked to complete the performance task.

As described above, performance tasks are usually given as summative tasks at the end of the unit. However, to complete a performance task successfully, students need to be able to integrate the knowledge and skills they learned in the corresponding unit and use them freely. Therefore, it is crucial to give the students an outlook at the beginning of the unit regarding what sort of performance tasks they will be doing by the end of the unit. Furthermore, effective teaching should also guide students to think about the knowledge and skills they have learned in each class in relation to the performance tasks. In addition, teachers should implement measures to motivate students since performance tasks are challenging.

In her teaching practice, Ms. Mifuji made her students hold concrete images by employing different measures after explaining the performance task at the beginning of the unit. These measures included showing recordings of TV programmes on topics she wanted the students to think about and giving examples of standpoints and situations in which examination was required. To begin with, the setting that she gave for the task was associated with the House of Representatives election that was to take place in the near future; this could be seen as a measure she used to motivate the students.

Additionally, worksheets such as the one displayed in Figure 10.6 were employed during the daily classes. The worksheets were used to verify the important knowledge

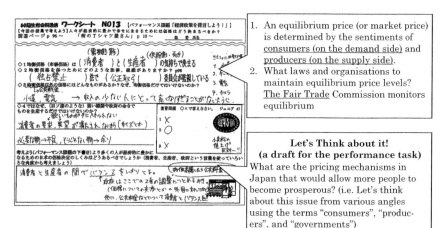

*Figure 10.6* A worksheet example

Source: Cf. Mifuji, 2010, p. 34. A figure from is used in the top half of this worksheet.

that could be used when engaging in a performance task. There was a column at the end of the worksheet in which the students were asked to write a section of a performance task rough draft.

### 3–2  Hold a debate session and organise ideas using a blackboard

In order for students to acquire abilities to engage in performance tasks, it is effective to strategically implement opportunities in classes where students express what they think or exchange their ideas with others. Ms. Mifuji herself also incorporated discussions held in various formats (i.e., debate sessions, discussions and presentations) in small groups or the entire class during her teaching guidance.

In the case of the economy unit, this measure took the form of a debate session within the mock debate programme that existed in the context of the performance task. In this debate session, the class was divided into groups of six or seven students in accordance with Stance A or B for each of the three topics so that each student could participate at least once as a 'Diet member' (see Figure 10.4). Figure 10.7 indicates the flow of the debate session, and Figure 10.8 depicts how the class looked during the session.

Teachers aid the students' thinking process by organising, on the blackboard, the keywords that appear in students' statements during the discussion session. For example, for the first topic 'Reduction of economic disparity', the debate between 'Stance A: Proceed with further free-competition' and 'Stance B: Reinforce social security' ended with the content shown in Figure 10.9 on the blackboard.

---

(1) Present one's own statements (write the statements on an A-3 sheet of paper and present them).
(Strategy time: Think within the group what kind of questions and refutations to present to the other group).
(2) Question the other party.
(3) Respond to the other party's questions.
(4) Both parties give opinions to each other.
(5) Receive questions and opinions from participants playing the role of the general public.
(The 'general public' participants are to make statements after clarifying their standpoints, which can range from a housewife in charge of the household finances to a high school student who became unable to attend school, a large corporation, SME, millionaire, and farmers).
(6) Each group responds to the questions and opinions that have been posed.
(7) Based on the content of the discussions, make a summary proposal.
(8) Summarise the students' reflections on the activity in the worksheet.

---

*Figure 10.7* The flow of the debate session within the economy unit

Source: Cf. Mifuji, 2010

*Figure 10.8* Image of a debate session in progress

Source: Cf. Mifuji, 2010

**<TV FY> Propose an Economic Policy!**
**How should we deal with economic disparity?**

A. Further Increase Free
   Competition!
   - Support enterprises and
   revitalize them.

B. Enhance Social Security
   - Support the working poor!

Economic          <u>Fulfillment of</u            Business
recovery      >   <u>Welfare Policy</u>    >     Development

Minimal level of                      Prioritisation of work
life security                         sharing schemes

◎Tax allocation                 What are we going to do
◎Livelihood support             about these issues?

*Figure 10.9* Blackboard notes that organised the opinions of Stances A and B

Source: Mifuji, 2010, p. 37

During this debate session, Stance A began with the statement, 'It is important to earn more through free competition. It is important to support companies to revitalise them rather than allocate the money to welfare', while Stance B said, 'It is precedent to support people who want to work but cannot after being made unable to do so, or working poor people who are not paid what they should be'. In the debate section, the students representing Stance B challenged those representing Stance A with the question, 'What kind of corporations would you assist? Even though you mentioned "revitalisation", since free competition is the principal law (as a philosophy under capitalism), wouldn't it be difficult to make this decision?' The Stance A students refuted this by saying, 'However, if free competition isn't revitalised, the budget allocated to welfare could not be generated. Therefore, you have to improve the economy before welfare'.

Many questions and opinions were raised that seemed plausible in the real world. For example, a student whose role was to represent the elderly stated, 'I am worried about my future livelihood if you don't strengthen the welfare system because I am an elderly person living on my pension'. Another student wondered, 'Because I am rich, I am asked to pay a lot of taxes as a high-income earner (due to the progressive taxation system) but what do the Diet members think?'

Ultimately, the Stance B students gave the concrete proposal that 'Constructing a work-sharing structure should be examined as a first priority even within a free-competition'. The Stance A students stated, 'The economy needs to be revitalised so that people can work while their bare minimum livelihood has been guaranteed'.

Although Stances A and B at first seemed to be in contradicting positions, it became evident from the notes on the blackboard that the two sides shared the view that the minimum level of life security for citizens should be the priority. At the end of the class, a question arose regarding how to distribute tax money and maintain livelihood in order to prevent more people from hardship experiencing additional hardship. These questions became an opportunity for other students who did not end up making a statement to form their own opinions.

After the debate session, the students wrote drafts and were then asked to further work on their drafts to complete a final copy. During this time, the teacher distributed a rubric, which the students used for self-assessment and modification of their draft. Furthermore, in order for the students to be able to exhibit their ability to use resources, the teachers created and distributed printouts that combined resources such as graphs and maps that the students could cite. The students cut out sections they needed from the printouts and cited them to complete their Policy Proposal Report.

## Conclusion

Presently, the significance of employing performance tasks for fostering abilities to think, form judgements and express oneself is gaining attention in Japan. The UbD proposes a way of developing performance tasks and creating an effective curriculum design under a long-term outlook for developing the abilities to think, form judgements and express oneself.

However, in Japan, it is not easy to have each student develop abilities to handle performance tasks, as the class sizes are larger than in the US. For example, it is virtually impossible to give individual guidance to all students using a format such as a debate session. Therefore, Ms. Mifuji provided guidance that developed the students' thoughts by combining the discussions held in small groups with those held as a whole class. Having the teacher organise the students' words was shown to be an effective method for giving associations and structures to the student's opinions and developing their thoughts.

## References

Director-General, Elementary and Secondary Education Bureau, the Ministry of Education, Culture, Sports, Science and Technology. (2010). *On improvements of learning assessment and cumulative guidance record of school children in elementary, middle, and high schools and special-needs schools (notice)* [Sho-gakko, chu-gakko, koto-gakko oyobi tokubetsu shien gakko ni okeru jido seito no gakusyu hyoka oyobi sido yoroku no kaizen-tou ni tuite]. Retrieved June 8, 2016, from http://www.mext.go.jp/b_menu/hakusho/nc/1292898.htm.

Erickson, H.L. (2008). *Stirring the Head, Heart, and Soul: Redefining Curriculum, Instruction, and Concept-Based Learning* (3rded). Thousand Oaks: CA, Corwin Press.

McTighe, J. & Ferrara, S. (1998). *Assessing Learning in the Classroom.* Washington DC: National Education Association.

McTighe, J. & Wiggins, G. (2004). *Understanding by Design Professional Development Workbook.* Alexandria: Association for Supervision and Curriculum Development (ASCD).

Mifuji, A. (2010). "Key points for guidance for performance tasks". In Mifuji, A. & Nishioka, K. (Eds.), *How to approach performance assessment: Social studies curriculum and lessons* [Performance hyoka ni do torikumuka: Tyu-gakko syakai-ka no curriculum to jugyou zukuri]. Tokyo: Nipponhyojun, pp. 30–43.

Mifuji, A. & Nishioka, K. (2010). *How to approach performance assessment: Social studies curriculum and lessons* [Performance hyoka ni do torikumuka: Tyu-gakko syakai-ka no curriculum to jugyou zukuri]. Tokyo: Nipponhyojun.

Nishioka, K. (2003). *Portfolio assessment utilised in subjects and integrated study* [Kyoka to sogo ni ikasu portfolio hyoka-hou]. Tokyo: Toshobunka.

Nishioka, K. (2008). "What is a 'backward design'? ['Gyakumuki-sekkei' towa nan-ika?]" In Nishioka, K. (Ed.), *Securing solid scholastic abilities using a 'backward design'* ['Gyakumuki-sekkei' de tashikana gakuryoku wo hosyosuru]. Tokyo: Meiji Tosho, pp. 9–32.

Nishioka, K. (2009a). "Issues surrounding academic achievement in Japan: Examining the 2008 revisions of the National Courses of Study". In Japanese Educational Research Association (JERA) (Ed.), *Educational studies in Japan*, No.3, Tokyo: JERA, pp. 5–16.

Nishioka, K. (2009b). "How to develop and make use of a performance task: The positive aspects of the theory of *understanding by design* and how to read this book [Performance kadai no tsukuri-kata to ikashi-kata: 'Gyakumuki-sekkei'-ron no miryoku to honsyo no yomi-kata]". In Nishioka, K. & Tanaka, K. (Eds.), *Lessons and assessments that foster 'ability to use knowledge and skills': Practices at middle schools* ["Katsuyosuru chikara" wo sodateru jugyou to hyoka: Chu-gakko]. Tokyo: Gakuji Shuppan, pp. 8–18.

Wiggins, G. (1998). *Educative Assessment: Designing Assessment to Inform and Improve Student Performance.* San Francisco: Jossey-Bass.

Wiggins, G. & McTigher, J. (1998). *Understanding by Design*, 1st Edition. Alexandria: Association for Supervision and Curriculum Development (ASCD).

Wiggins, G. & McTighe, J. (2005). *Understanding by design*, Expanded 2nd Edition. Alexandria: Association for Supervision and Curriculum Development (ASCD). [Rikai wo motarasu Curriculum sekkei: "Gyakumuki-sekkei" no riron to houhou] (K. Nishioka, Trans., 2012). Tokyo: Nipponhyojun.

# Chapter 11

# Conclusion

*Kanae Nishioka*

This book has introduced practices of curriculum, guidance and assessment in Japan by looking back on their post-war history. Chapter 1 introduced four perspectives to analyse the status of academic ability, as well as the idea of lesson study (Jugyou Kenkyuu). Here, let us reflect on the main points of the other chapters one more time and consider what part of educational practice in Japan goes beyond lesson study.

Part 1 focused on the curriculum. Whilst the curriculum is controlled by the government, various imaginative and original ideas have been put into practice in schools in Japan (Chapter 2). The driving force behind their implementation includes not only government training but also school-based teacher training, as well as training in which teachers participate on a voluntary basis. In particular, the initiatives of the non-governmental educational research movement, in which teachers voluntarily participate to pursue better educational practices along with researchers, is worth noting. In the United States, for example, certain theories proposed by theorists are provided at training to be popularised. In Japan, however, the non-governmental educational research movement functions as a network to consolidate the knowledge on practices across the country and has begun a cycle in which researchers consider the consolidated knowledge from a theoretical perspective and the knowledge is then verified in the field.

Under such circumstances, various debates took place within and between non-governmental educational research organisations, resulting in theoretical and practical advancements. What became a major contention among them was whether to take child-centred education or discipline-centred education as the principle for organising the curriculum (Chapter 3). Original core-curriculum theories, the *Suidohoshiki* (the way of water course) method, and *Kasetsu-jikken-jugyou* (Hypothesis-Verification-Through Experimentation Learning System) were created learning from theories developed overseas such as those of Dewey and Bruner. It can be said that the fact the 1998 revision of the National Courses of Study (NCS) introduced the Period for Integrated Study (PFIS) symbolises that the policy emphasised the establishment of time for children to inquire on their own in the curriculum. Furthermore, the 'PISA shock' of 2004 led to the position that the abilities to utilise knowledge and skill to think, judge and express oneself are important elements in each subject. This can be recognised as something that showed the direction to develop the ability to use knowledge and skills, which assists inquires in the PFIS.

Under these debates, theoretical studies to consider the type of educational objectives (academic achievements and qualities and competencies to be developed in school) may have also advanced (Chapter 4). In the debate between child-centred education and discipline-centred education, academic achievement model theories were proposed one after the other with respect to how knowledge and attitude should be associated in terms of academic achievement. Although positioning academic achievement as an educational objective itself was questioned during the era of 'relaxed education', improving comprehensive learning abilities is widely pursued today. Furthermore, the focus of debate now has come down to how to position qualities and competencies, such as general cross-subject skills, in the curriculum. It is important to understand not only the elements of qualities and competencies but also their qualitative depth and to learn once more from not only subjects but also the history of practices implemented in life guidance and extra-curricular activities.

Focusing on guidance, Part 2 summarised again the historical efforts to improve lesson study as well as practices that go beyond lesson study. As pointed out in Chapter 5, the lesson studies J. W. Stigler and J. Hiebert (1999) introduced in *The Teaching Gap* (Free Press) are only part of the works done by teachers in Japan in pursuit of improved practice. In Japan, there is a culture of recording practice in which practices, which are viewed on a longer-term basis from teachers' perspective, are recorded and shared among teachers. The two methods have complemented each other and supported teachers' efforts to creatively improve educational practices. This was tied to the transformation of educational practice from teaching to learning during the 1990s, and a framework to view it from the dichotomous oppositional scheme between technical expert and reflective practitioner was proposed. In order to overcome this dichotomous oppositional scheme, it is necessary to re-evaluate the value of design orientation and creativity-dominance linage and aim to create lessons as art.

Chapter 6 introduced four excellent educators who sought a link between life and education as well as between science and education. Yoshio Ito, a *seikatsu-tsudurikata* (life writing) teacher (who teaches about life through composition), analysed how children struggled and identified a possibility to link the logic of subject matter and the logic of real life. Kihaku Saito, who followed the school of liberal education that began in the Taisho era, stressed the role of the teacher in passing down rich culture through lessons and laid the foundation for research on educational methods by advancing the study on thought-provoking questions. Kazuaki Shoji, who proposed the Hypothesis-Verification Through Experimentation Learning System, pursued lessons to teach students how to gain deep understanding by doing *nobori-ori* (going up and down) between real-life knowledge and scientific knowledge. Yasutaro Tamada, an exemplary practitioner from the Association of Science Education, actualised a practice in which guidance and learning were implemented by clarifying the attainment targets, devising instructional materials and a guidance process based on the targets, facilitating cooperation and the individualisation of teaching (learning?) and utilising formative assessment.

In Chapter 7, a teacher's competency in organising a lesson as drama was examined by considering that there is a tradition to pursue lessons that are hammered out by pooling each individual's ideas. There are five decision points in planning a lesson: goals and objectives in education; instructional materials and learning tasks; the flow of lesson and the structure of the forum; skills, techniques and technology of the lesson; and educational assessment. In addition, it is important for teachers to carry out the entire process of planning, implementing and reflecting on a lesson on their own in order to hone their competency.

Part 3 examined the improvement of practice centred on assessment. The concept of evaluation was imported from the United States to Japan after World War II. However, it took a long time to establish the understanding that assessment is an activity to help improve education rather than to appraise children. The cumulative guidance record had long used relative assessment; it was the 2001 revision of the cumulative guidance record that finally adopted objective-referenced assessment. Then, the authentic assessment theory was introduced and, as portfolio assessment and performance assessment gained popularity, the importance of encouraging children to self-assess and ensuring children's participation in educational assessment began attracting attention (Chapter 8).

Chapter 9 introduced cases of practices that utilised portfolio assessment in the PFIS. Portfolio assessment is an approach in which teachers encourage students to self-assess how their learning should be through the creation of a portfolio while the teachers themselves assess each student's learning activities as well as their own teaching activities. Ms. Hiroko Miyamoto defined a broad theme to allow children to take various approaches and supported children's inquiry by holding group conferences and organising the details of class discussions on the blackboard. Portfolios can play an essential role in helping the teacher understand each child's learning progress and plan appropriate guidance.

Chapter 10 introduced practices that incorporate performance tasks into teaching subjects. The term 'performance task' refers to a complex task that requires comprehensive mastery of various forms of knowledge and skills. Ms. Asami Mifuji, who applied the *Understanding by Design* (Wiggins & McTighe, 2005) theory to social studies in junior high school, devised a form of guidance by developing performance tasks corresponding to the essential questions, structurally arranging unit guidance, and organising students' thoughts on the blackboard at a discussion session.

As shown in the above summary, while the lesson study in the format of an open house and pre- and post-conferences occupies a central position in the efforts of educators in Japan to improve practices, that is not all. There is also a culture to understand practices over a long span by recording and sharing them.

Furthermore, non-governmental educational research organisations have created a cycle in which teachers examine each other's practices and theorise about them, and then the theory is verified in practice. Teachers and researchers have also proactively learned from the findings of research overseas, especially in the United States, and drawn on their learning to create practices that are distinctive to Japan.

Researchers play the role of promoting the cycle of developing a theory from practice and then spreading the theory to put into practice. In addition, teachers themselves develop effective ways of teaching by proactively participating in a variety of networks and utilising various theories.

For example, Ms. Hiroko Miyamoto, introduced in Chapter 9, had studied the practice of Hama Omura for a long time. Hama Omura was the teacher who developed the unit method of teaching, wherein children learn by their own initiative, after World War II (see Chapter 5). Upon undertaking the practice of the PFIS, Ms. Miyamoto learned from the author (Nishioka) about portfolio assessment and the teaching method of organising children's thoughts by writing them on the blackboard. The technique of organising children's thoughts on the blackboard was imparted by the author, who had learned about the practice at the Elementary School Attached to Nara Women's University, which has been a traditional child-centred school since the beginning of the New Education Movement during the Taisho period (see also Chapter 5). Ms. Miyamoto succeeded in effectively utilising portfolios by using a combination of papers and class discussions, in addition to individual and group dialogues, to hold more substantial conferences.

In addition, Ms. Asami Mifuji, introduced in Chapter 10, has participated in one of the non-governmental educational research organisations, *Syoshinokai* (the Society for Achieving the Original Spirit of Social Studies), which pursues child-centred approaches to lessons (see Chapter 5). Learning from the organisation, Ms. Mifuji explored lessons in which students debate. Later, she came across *Understanding by Design* through the author (Nishioka) and became committed to developing practices that incorporate performance tasks. By becoming conscious of the structure of knowledge, Ms. Mifuji became capable of organising discussions among students while directing their attention to the essential content of the subject. Incidentally, Ms. Mifuji's practice also included creative guidance such as using worksheets and organising children's thoughts on the blackboard.

One underlying factor for lesson study being talked about in the mainstream in Japan is that the era in which the curriculum was tightly controlled by the national government lasted a long time. However, once the 1998 revision of the NCS emphasised inventive approaches at each school and introduced the PFIS, the momentum increased for the teachers' movement to develop units and longer-term guidance plans. Furthermore, a new development emerged to improve guidance and the curriculum by devising assessment methods in response to the introduction of objective-referenced assessment in the NCS revised in 2001.

In Japan, where class sizes are large, it is not easy to provide attentive guidance to a diverse group of children. However, teachers in Japan have devised a unique lesson style in which ideas are worked out in groups by taking advantage of the children's diversity. Such creativity of teachers has been demonstrated in their creation and improvement of assessment methods such as portfolio assessment and performance assessment, developing units, and even developing long-term guidance plans. I would like to emphasise that teachers' creativity is the gem of Japanese educational practices that we want to communicate overseas.

## References

Stigler, J. W. & Hiebert, J. (1999). *The teaching gap: Best ideas from the world's teachers for improving education in the classroom.* New York: Free Press.

Wiggins, G. & McTighe, J. (2005). *Understanding by design,* Expanded 2nd Edition. Alexandria: Association for Supervision and Curriculum Development (ASCD). [Rikai wo motarasu Curriculum sekkei: "Gyakumuki-sekkei" no riron to houhou] (K. Nishioka, Trans., 2012). Tokyo: Nipponhyojun.

# Index